Adaptive Education

An Inquiry-Based Institution

ROBERT VANWYNSBERGHE
AND ANDREW C. HERMAN

UNIVERSITY OF TORONTO PRESS
Toronto Buffalo London

ISBN 978-1-4426-3040-6

∞ Printed on acid-free, 100% post-consumer recycled paper with vegetable-based inks.

___

Library and Archives Canada Cataloguing in Publication

VanWynsberghe, Robert M., author
Adaptive education : an inquiry-based institution / Robert VanWynsberghe
and Andrew C. Herman.

Includes bibliographical references and index.
ISBN 978-1-4426-3040-6 (bound)

1. Education – Research. 2. Education – Experimental methods. 3. Teaching
– Research. 4. Educational change. I. Herman, Andrew C., 1988–, author II.
Title.

LB1028.24.V35 2016   370.72   C2015-907179-8

___

University of Toronto Press acknowledges the financial assistance to its
publishing program of the Canada Council for the Arts and the Ontario
Arts Council, an agency of the Government of Ontario.

**Canada Council
for the Arts**

**Conseil des Arts
du Canada**

**ONTARIO ARTS COUNCIL
CONSEIL DES ARTS DE L'ONTARIO**
an Ontario government agency
un organisme du gouvernement de l'Ontario

Funded by the
Government
of Canada

Financé par le
gouvernement
du Canada

Contents

vi   Contents

Figures

ADAPTIVE EDUCATION

An Inquiry-Based Institution

1 Introduction

Few teachers spend time wondering about the latest scientific findings, even when the research could improve their practical approach. Mainstream policy makers sometimes respond to this gap between research and practice by punishing teachers who underperform and rewarding teachers who are especially successful, in an attempt to incentivize professional development.[1] But blaming teachers in this case is wrongheaded. There is very little infrastructure in place to communicate empirical results to front-line educators in our schools, few opportunities for teachers to participate in research themselves, and only weak norms to encourage the development of an evidence-based profession. What we need to do instead is to rethink how our education system is put together, and to rebuild the institutional structure from the bottom up.

This book is concerned with several interrelated questions. Why do we not use the education system as an empirical testing ground for the latest theories? How could we maximize educational quality by doing so?[2] Why is the teaching profession not based on scientific research or, at least, why does its scientific basis differ so dramatically from the scientific bases of professions such as medicine? How could we organize the school system to intervene more effectively in social issues such as obesity and sustainability? We could boil it down to this: education today is not a scientific enterprise, and this fact is holding us back.[3] Despite the millions of dollars governments invest every year in relevant research in the social sciences – in cognitive development, health literacy, knowledge exchange, and lifelong learning – much of the knowledge gained from that research fails to make an impact in the classroom. Pre-service teachers are not always trained to base their practice on inquiry, and many choose to disregard their training once they enter the field, opting instead to base their practice on gut feelings. Despite their good intentions, most teachers are generally disconnected from the research process and have limited resources to draw upon in any attempt to hone their craft. They are, in short, products of the structural constraints placed on them by our educational institutions. This concern is not new. In its mature form it goes back to early proponents of a science of education such as Edward Thorndike and John Dewey.[4] And although Dewey and his fellow pragmatists saw teaching as an art, they emphasized the importance of learning from research and practical wisdom. Even fifty years later, Dan Lortie's classroom ethnographies helped to keep the issue alive in the minds of policy makers and theorists alike.[5]

The educational system's failure to make use of scientific knowledge in schools is stupefying in light of the fact that other institutions regularly piggyback on that same universal educational system to implement their own empirically justified social policy. Medical systems (with the help of regional and national governments) use schools to administer vaccinations to nearly the entire population, limit the ability of children to spread disease by installing new technologies and infrastructure, and combat obesity by encouraging exercise regimens. Governments reduce intercultural tensions through innovative curricula and field trips designed to familiarize students with different belief systems. Without public schools, a number of such evidence-based social programs that target whole populations would be unfeasible.

In an attempt to address the disconnect between research and practice, we offer an alternative institutional structure for education that we call "adaptive education." It incorporates research processes within the school system, changes the daily routines of teachers and students, and adjusts the professional expectations (with appropriate supports) for educators. We have tried to make these reform proposals plausible to both policy makers and users of the institution.

Increasingly in contemporary society, when we talk about letting research guide policy, critics invoke the spectre of scientism.[6] That is, they worry about the creation of public discourse that is disproportionately moderated and influenced by science and its proponents at the expense of commonly held opinions. They fear that, because empirical data do not support more popular opinions, a scientific elite could disenfranchise ordinary citizens by foisting unattractive policies onto them.

But incorporating knowledge production into discussions about public policy should not lead to the loss of public voice. Even the most local of actors can be involved in the research process, and there are good reasons for encouraging them to be. At the very least, different opinions and experiences serve as preliminary data points that we can use to generate theories. But more importantly, local actors are best acquainted with the particularities and nuances of their own social context. They are well placed to uncover, by trial and error, effective habits that can be positively emulated in public institutions.

Some curricular content issues – such as the origins of humans or, perhaps more contemporaneously, climate change – are linked to belief systems that might compete with, if not transcend, data in some ways. The point is that the relative weight applied to evidence in these cases is not just a problem for a data-gathering institution such as the one we propose; in teaching evolution as a fact in science classes, we juxtapose evidence with the cultural belief systems of some, and, in doing so, violate or challenge those belief systems. Indeed this is one way we claim to make use of evidence in the curriculum without installing a scientistic regime.

Better Data and Customized Interventions

Among the many suggestions public figures bandy about for how to increase educational quality, two stand out: helping teachers improve their overall approach, and helping them better target the needs of individual students. We see these goals taking centre stage in debates over classroom size, rewards to motivate teachers, teacher training, and school infrastructure or budgets. Our proposal works by targeting both goals simultaneously. The additional data generated through research in the educational institution would give teachers the resources both to improve their existing techniques and to customize their (empirically grounded) methods to better address the individual needs of their students.

These reforms would mark an improvement over existing practice. To understand the limitations of existing practice, consider the nineteenth-century origins of modern education, which stressed universality at the expense of individual differences. Although early reformers in the United States and Europe drew from different philosophical traditions and from cross-national comparisons in their efforts to modernize school systems, by the late nineteenth century educators were emulating the revolutionary model of education that had been introduced in Prussia. The Prussian model represents the earliest attempt to transplant the lessons of the Industrial Revolution onto the design of public education and, as such, illustrates how institutional change can mirror cultural change.[7]

Were it not for Napoleon's defeat of the Prussian army at Jena in 1806, the institution of universal compulsory education might never have been implemented as widely as it was. Jena was catastrophic for Prussia: French forces crushed its professional army, and the country fell under French rule. In the aftermath of the battle, the philosopher Johann Fichte argued that lack of discipline accounted for the national defeat. Along with others, he advocated reforming Prussia's education system by enforcing its compulsory aspects, with the goal of developing obedience and nationalism in the Prussian public.[8] The resultant model was based on the factory model of production introduced by the Industrial Revolution. Students were divided into groups according to age, and each grade was assigned standard curricula, allowing teachers to focus on the mass production of educated citizens instead of tailoring classes to individual needs. It should not be difficult for readers to recognize the influence this model exerted on school systems around the world.

These reforms, however, were not the inevitable product of the Industrial Revolution; had they been, they might have been introduced sooner. By 1809, when Prussian minister of education Wilhelm von Humboldt introduced the new structure, the factory model of production had existed for more than fifty years. During that time, several other countries had enacted compulsory education without imitating the production line. Had the Battle of Jena not forced a radical reconsideration of the institutional arrangement in Prussia – that is, had it not created conditions favourable for dramatic reform – the Prussian model of education might not have been created, and its countless imitators would have looked elsewhere for inspiration. Another country eventually might have developed a facsimile of mass-production methods in education, but at the time that was anything but a foregone conclusion. In fact, reformers in other countries faced severe backlashes over their efforts to import Prussian education, and were successful only because of historical contingency and their conviction that the Prussian model represented a more effective and efficient school system. A country in crisis exemplified new ways of thinking, providing traction for reformers in other jurisdictions.

To understand the importance of this development, consider that education today is still premised on the assembly line. We separate students by age into production stages that we call grade levels, and at each stage we assign them to one worker, a teacher, who specializes in performing the tasks related to specific age groups or subject matter. We call these tasks pedagogy and curriculum, each of which is geared to the psychological and social development of specific age groups. Over time students are passed along to the next specialized worker and the next, until they graduate with the certification that they have completed the assembly process associated with that level of schooling.

This makes the school system sound dehumanizing, and surely some students experience it that way. In fact, nowhere are students treated merely as passive factory inputs. Education today is generally understood to be a collaborative process between teachers, students, and their peers.[9] Information is not imposed on the minds of pupils; rather, learning requires their participation and deliberate activity. When we suggest that education resembles the industrial production line, we are referring not to the activities that constitute its practice, but to its underlying structural design, which informs and constrains the possibilities of that practice.

Factories are efficient because, instead of one worker performing twenty tasks, diluting the expertise of an individual employee, each worker specializes in one task, which makes that worker supremely effective at his or her job. For this reason we assign teachers to one age group or one subject. We populate high schools, for example, with thirty or more teachers who are especially skilled in their own instructional field (chemistry, literature, physical health, and so on), with the goal of improving the overall educational experience.

But the finely crafted routines that allow for the raw efficiency of the factory depend on homogeneous inputs. Imagine we are building toy cars, and that one worker specializes in installing their axles and tires. (Parents everywhere can attest to how maddeningly difficult this can be.) Each time misshapen axles and tires appear, the assembly line slows down as the worker is pulled out of her repetitive mode to deal with the specific needs of the particular piece. To avoid this problem, most factories dispose of irregular inputs before they reach the assembly line. Schools at all levels face a parallel dilemma. Students who break the predetermined mould – who are irregular inputs, in production terminology – whether because of environmental circumstances, psychological development in childhood, or other behavioural factors, disrupt the smooth functioning of the assembly line. As a result, despite the best intentions of teachers and administrators, they receive an inferior education, feel out of place, and sometimes drop out entirely.

We are not suggesting that the design of the modern education system should be abandoned entirely. On the contrary, it has many redeeming aspects. As citizens and planners, we appreciate that it produces respectable outcomes at a reasonable price – at least compared to the alternatives. Its potential to reach every child and adult makes it possible to develop an intelligent and knowledgeable workforce, provide recognized qualifications to help certify the skill level of prospective employees, enforce and implement mandated legislation such as vaccination schedules, and exert some level of control over the socialization process (for better or for worse). When economic and political pressures arise that demand new ways of thinking and new skills, we turn to our education system to provide them. Individuals return to school after losing their jobs, hoping to find and pursue new possibilities for their lives. Governments call for an increased focus on science, technology, engineering, and medicine in the curriculum to prepare the country for change. In developing countries, universal education brings new groups – women, minorities, marginalized social classes – into the social fold, so that economic productivity can increase through an influx of skilled workers.

Without sacrificing these positive aspects, we believe it is possible to mitigate the negative effects of the factory line by using standards that have already been deployed in other institutions, most of which are based on a similar factory ethos. Hospitals direct patients according to partial diagnoses that are made at the moment of admittance, giving them access to the most relevant specialists. Mental health professionals have similar pre-sorting measures to maximize effectiveness, referring patients to group therapy sessions, one-on-one intervention, or their family doctor. The same kind of pre-sorting is sometimes used in education to place students in different school situations based on achievement or future goals. Germany's school system represents the most prominent example of this method, generally known as tracking or streaming. However, pre-sorting of students remains controversial in many countries, including Canada and the United States, as it has the potential to limit social mobility and individual autonomy.

We argue that customization need not rely on moving students into various environments according to previous evaluations, as exemplified in the German system. Instead, institutions could adapt classroom techniques to meet the needs of students who enrol through regular, non-sorting processes, turning the instructor into something of an empirically backed artisan. To mitigate the factory metaphor, this model would give teachers more responsibilities. Although we recognize this as a potential problem, it would allow the reform process to be simplified by introducing fewer structural changes to the existing system. Customization in the classroom can take many forms, and we do not intend to commit ourselves dogmatically to any one. The special education system in Finland uses this approach by combining a battery of diagnostic tools to assess pre-school students for learning, developmental, or behavioural difficulties. Customization plays an important role in our proposal because improving the quality of education depends on adapting classroom techniques to individual needs. People with varying characteristics respond differently to stimuli in school. Some techniques are best suited for boys who like sports, teenagers with divorced parents, or minority students who live in the inner city. Applying the same techniques to seven-year-old Caucasian girls who live in the suburbs will not necessarily have detrimental effects, but it will likely be less effective than other approaches. If efficiency dictates that we model institutions on the production line, quality demands that the production line be capable of handling diverse inputs.

To allow for this level of customization, in whatever form, we need to weave more and better data into the institutional fabric. Teachers and policy makers can determine which techniques to use in which situations only through an extensive knowledge base founded on continuing scientific research. Although valuable on an individual level, personal experience is insufficient for this purpose because there are no convenient ways of sharing and validating it. Educators need data on interventions that speak to specific outcomes and that detail the salient characteristics of ideal candidates for those interventions. The former quality is necessary both to align the method with predetermined lesson goals and to form realistic expectations about results. The latter makes it possible to distinguish between approaches that produce similar outcomes but have different levels of effectiveness in different populations.

Because changing social and cultural conditions can make techniques more or less effective over time, these data need to be viewed guardedly and re-evaluated periodically (and developed comparatively if this kind of institution is to cooperate internationally). This is not to say that empirically based education will lead to an institutional bloodletting, but that changing preconceptions and social conditions might limit or enhance the benefits or drawbacks of a particular approach. For instance, norms surrounding masculinity today might discourage teenage boys from participating in activities such as ballet and yoga, regardless of benefits ranging from improved balance and flexibility to better emotional control. Over time such practices might become more acceptable within the masculine repertoire, bringing changes to the expected outcomes associated with educational techniques dependent on them.

Given the number of variables that affect educational outcomes and the rate of social change, we believe it is important to develop the scientific basis for educational reform and practice. Although this includes disseminating research findings to practitioners, it equally involves building the institutional trappings to support the formation of cumulative knowledge. It is not enough to encourage teachers to engage in lifelong learning or to haphazardly provide reading materials that outline new findings. The entire system should be designed so that teaching and learning are implicitly, if not explicitly, understood by everyone involved to be empirical issues.

For this reason our proposal for adaptive education centres around the creation of an institutional arm that focuses on undertaking research and organizing findings, involving researchers, instructors, and students (in addition to community and family members) in the research process. Institutional contexts shape professional norms and public expectations. By transforming them we make it more likely that changes to regular practice will occur.

Experimenting with Education

Few educators would dispute the need to increase both the volume and the quality of data; the more taxing issue is to find ways to collect, analyse, and turn them into concrete recommendations for best practices. Although the work of researchers and education scholars has contributed, and continues to contribute, to our understanding of teaching and learning, the process remains informal and unorganized, limited to the valuable but inefficient functions of library databases and journal volumes. Findings are not always communicated to the people who could use them, despite the claim of faculties of education to the contrary, and the massive potential for research in schools across the country is underexploited.

We argue that educational institutions should be the site of continuous experimentation and, perhaps more pointedly, that education itself should be seen as one large and continuous experiment. Efforts are already underway to move in this direction, but they have not yet gone far enough. Most federal government funding for research comes under the rubric of grants to stimulate research into reducing the cost of innovation. Although the government's real motivation is to improve Canada's ability to compete with other countries in an era of the rapid application of new technologies, it has also created space for a productive marriage of corporate and academic cultures in various disciplines and sectors. In this research and development policy, the educational sector is a suitable field for innovation activities.

The gold standard university–industry partnership in Canada is Research in Motion (RIM), the makers of Blackberry. As the story goes, ideas about wireless communication were generated in the halls of the University of Waterloo, but it was Bay Street that ultimately sponsored the testing and growth of the relevant technologies. RIM was able to cultivate a relationship with the University of Waterloo, which provided a steady stream of bright student interns and graduates who helped the company innovate and, for a time, rule the sector. Now the federal government wishes to enable this happy marriage with sliding scales of funding that increase as the experiment grows in size and validity.

In the United States, the Department of Education's (DOE) Office of Innovation and Improvement is ambitious in its efforts to support innovation. Its primary aim is to identify quickly and scale up possible solutions to emerging or persistent educational challenges, and it makes strategic investments in innovative educational programs. One such program is the Office of Investing in Innovation, which responds to enrolment and retention problems by supporting non-traditional solutions via educational television and other digital media, whose audiences can be the very young or the disadvantaged. Investing in Innovation has invested almost US$135 million to support the expansion of effective educational solutions since it started in 2010.

It would be extremely beneficial to increase the scale of successful pilot educational research efforts, and the interest is there. Thousands of schools are eager to improve student performance, millions of students are hoping to secure an attractive job or a place in a post-secondary program, and many social scientists lack the funding to carry out their research programs. But educational institutions cannot write a blank cheque to support scientific advancement, and financial support for research programs is rarely reliable. National or state governments often mandate institutional budgets; political and other forces act in unpredictable ways; governments change, and so do the winds of public sentiment. Although we would like to see funding levels for education increase, or at least hold steady, given the political climate in favour of privatizing education that is evident in both Canada and the United States, we should expect decreasing budgets across the sector.

At the same time, as educators committed to improving our system and practices, it seems poor form to throw our arms in the air and abandon the field to fiscal policy makers. So, we argue, there are good reasons to think that investment in innovation is offset at least partly by the validation of techniques that cost less or that increase economic output in the long run. To quibble about budget crunches when it comes to innovation is short-sighted at best. Officials can be financially savvy while still aggressively pursuing improvements to the education system.

We also think that contemporary approaches to educational research betray an overly narrow definition of what counts as an experiment. Although we recognize scientific research as the gold standard for inquiry, we also argue that there is a wealth of on-the-ground experience that should not be ignored, as organizational theorists have rightly pointed out. Teachers, community leaders, parents, and even students themselves "experiment" with education all the time. They play around with their schedules, lesson plans, and study techniques to find useful ways to approach the situations that arise in their regular activities. Traditionally, educational institutions have barely acknowledged this potential source of wisdom. Those who want to share their ideas for improving the educational experience are directed to suggestion boxes, e-mail addresses, or their local school trustee.

Recently, however, there has been renewed interest in the input from so-called master teachers – elementary or secondary school teachers whose advanced professional preparation and teaching experience qualifies them to assist in the preparation of student teachers or teacher interns, to give guidance to inexperienced teachers, or to coordinate and lead teams of teachers. This innovation has inspired "master teacher programs," which tend to be immersive and require participants to undertake a research study that culminates in a personal philosophical and/or methodological position on classroom practice. We see these programs as promising because they prepare graduates to contribute directly to education, foster learning in other kinds of organizations, or both.

Incorporating experience, inquiry, and reflection in teacher training is a move in the right direction, especially if it includes, as well, the idea of a central data repository. But we should be collecting regular feedback from teachers everywhere – masters and otherwise – on what is working and what is not. The daily experiments that are part of teachers' everyday practice are not controlled in the scientific sense, and neither are they carefully planned beforehand, so we cannot treat the insights they produce in the same way as we do findings from more rigorous educational research. But they can generate new questions, supply support for existing research, identify the blind spots in current theories, and direct us towards new avenues for study.

The Benefits of Adaptive Education

In many ways the primary benefits of the proposal we detail in this book align with what most consider the positive outcomes of education, but there are surprises, and these tend to coalesce around social and health benefits. We turn to these outcomes to support our argument for grounding teaching and learning more firmly on empirical evidence, and for using that evidence to customize the educational experience for students.

According to a recent publication of the Organisation for Economic Co-operation and Development, better education improves life expectancy: a thirty-year-old with post-secondary education can expect to live, on average, eight years longer than a high school graduate – that is, to die at eighty-three rather than at seventy-five.[10] Over his or her lifetime, this average university graduate will vote and engage in civic volunteering activities at a significantly higher rate than a non-graduate, and will report greater life satisfaction. These outcomes remain in place after controlling for income: education appears to offer alternative paths to the competencies, networks, and social standing that seem key to living well.

Post-secondary education also appears to sponsor the healthy behaviours that contribute to longevity. In the United States, a 2012 College Board study reported that only 8 per cent of people with a bachelor's degree or more smoked, compared with 25 per cent of those with a high school diploma or less. As well, obesity rates are lower among college graduates, which is likely attributable to the increased amount of time they spend exercising per week: nearly two-thirds of graduates of four-year colleges met minimum US federal guidelines for weekly physical activity, but only 38 per cent of those with no more than a high school diploma did so.

By reflecting societal norms and encouraging community involvement, education influences personal behaviour, fosters social consciousness, and ultimately changes society. Acquiring these social and personal skills and tools can help students achieve objectives that contribute to academic success and, ultimately, that appeal to employers. Secondary schools, for example, often have volunteer requirements that involve interacting with diverse groups of people. These experiences demand organization and discipline, which are key to post-secondary success and open the door to economic, social, and health benefits.

Our proposals build on these benefits by maximizing the educational experience for all age groups and all segments of society in two ways. First, we propose that a variety of stakeholders be engaged in the learning process. This would not only enhance the experience of students themselves; it would also allow the broader community to interact with and influence the next generation. By giving students the opportunity to meet and collaborate with the representatives of governments, courts, businesses, and other institutions, we would introduce them, first-hand, to the ways in which education transforms lives. For example, a seventeen-year-old who wanted to apply for a program in urban planning would meet stakeholders in an urban issue her class is studying, which would both test her interest and offer an experience that would improve her chances for admission and ultimate success in the urban planning program.

Second, we posit a model that would extend education beyond the four walls of the classroom and encourage students to engage with real-life problems, which would challenge their everyday learning habits. A student would learn how to ask and answer questions publicly and seek information from non-typical sources – for example, the student's exposure to homelessness might lead his or her family to support a shelter in their neighbourhood, while the student might go on to a lifetime of civic engagement with social issues. As adult educators know well, out-of-classroom and off-campus sites present students with learning opportunities dominated by everyday activities, and often expose them to patterns of behaviour that contribute to social problems. Imagine a school lesson that involved strolling through the mall to test the social studies teacher's claim that the mall works because it offers the thrill of consumption many times over in a short time. Finding support for this assertion, the student might develop a more open attitude to a variety of learning experiences and, as an adult, might enjoy a high level of life satisfaction due, in part, to an ongoing and genuine curiosity.

As designers of learning environments, teachers and others can implicitly craft experiences that disrupt the routines we call subjects or disciplines; for example, later on in this book, we discuss the use of theatre to inspire math appreciation. Making these connections adds intriguing and compelling dimensions to, say, the individual act of voting, which might lead students to imagine themselves entering the world of pundits and policy wonks, managing a network of acquaintances, or digesting the latest survey results on citizens' satisfaction with the current leader.

Of course, our main objective in putting forth this proposal for adaptive education is to improve the learning environment for students. However, in addition to offering learning advantages for both students and teachers, our model offers some practical, long-term employment advantages to the broader educational sector. Incorporating research into the fabric of the public education institution might provide new employment options for educators interested in combining research skills with an on-site presence in schools. Ultimately, these opportunities could be reflected in the options offered to pre-service and graduate students in faculties of education.

We believe our proposal is attractive on philosophical as well as on practical grounds. It addresses some key questions at the heart of the educational enterprise: How should the merits of the education system be evaluated? On whose authority should decisions about education be made? Who gets to identify problems and chart out where to go from here?

Following John Dewey and Roberto Unger, both of whom receive due attention later on, our model would let people decide some of the educational issues for themselves. Practice is tied to local context, and actors familiar with that context would be able to experiment with solutions and share their success or failure with others facing similar situations. To be successful, however, our model requires an organizational structure. The one we propose focuses as much on bottom-up influence as on top-down coordination, ensuring pathways for participation: people would be able to see their own perceived problems addressed, sometimes with their own ideas operating as the intervention.

Looking Forward

We coined the term "adaptive education" to refer to the institutional arrangement for education that emphasizes a commitment to research input. In the following chapters, we detail our proposal for an attachment to the existing institutional structure of education that is designed to generate and maintain this commitment across the school system from primary to post-secondary. This attachment, which we call the Epistemic Division, draws inspiration for its processes from the scientific method, Bayesian epistemology, and American pragmatism, especially as it would try to balance risk with benefit and uncertainty with confidence, while developing the scientific basis for education. Our use of Epistemic Division is meant to capture the new and organizational aspect of the effort to accumulate research findings and make advances in our understanding of education. For us, the term captures both the knowledge and the not-quite-knowledge pieces that we need to emphasize. The not-quite-knowledge refers to unconfirmed findings that await further study or are tangential to the specific project from which they are derived. The new structure would supplement and buttress the existing institution, rather than replace it. In addition to structural transformation, our proposal calls for new professional standards and daily routines in teaching and administration. We are convinced that, if the proposal were implemented in the real world, the cumulative changes would be substantial and encompassing.

A primary responsibility of the Epistemic Division would be to design research projects, and to collect and analyse the ensuing data. These projects would be organized to replicate earlier findings, and would develop according to prevailing understandings of education as well as the various policy and other contexts that affect the educational institution itself. Researchers would also draw on the experiences of local actors, as though they were preliminary data points, to validate existing theories and develop new ones. Committees tasked with evaluating the state of knowledge on a given topic and scaling research projects appropriately over time would handle decisions about replicating findings and incorporating more nuanced data. Classrooms and participants would be recruited and assigned according to the investment in the research and the risk involved in a project.

The collection and analysis of the data from these projects would be undertaken in a central repository that would operate as a database, allowing experts to assess the state of knowledge and identify directions for future research. Researchers' confidence in relationships posited by previous research is always expressed as a probability, and attempts to replicate these relationships results in fresh data that, in turn, helps to increase or decrease those confidence levels. Over time, some findings about teaching and learning would prove to be limited by historical contingency, and the institution (and the social sciences more broadly) would adapt accordingly.

A database of cutting-edge knowledge would also give teachers and administrators empirical evidence to support educational improvement, both directly, through powerful data-mining tools that allow individuals to assess their immediate circumstances in light of accumulated knowledge, and indirectly, through the publication of exciting developments, culminating in a standard best-practices manual that should be updated regularly. The availability of this information would make it possible to tailor educational practices to fit the needs of students, whether individually or in groups.

With added customization, the overall quality of our schools would increase, as students would be given not only personalized attention, but also a scientifically grounded learning experience. In a broader social context, policy makers would also have access to this database and to the wider educational research functions, so as to allow educational and social interventions around issues such as obesity or multiculturalism to be grounded in empirical data.

To accomplish these goals, we argue that the education profession needs to adopt new, research-driven standards. In our proposal, pre-service teacher training programs would include research components within the Epistemic Division. In addition, new or ongoing research projects would enlist pre-service teachers as research assistants. Practising teachers, meanwhile, would engage in regular discussion groups designed to elicit classroom experiences and generate preliminary data points for analysts. They might also gather feedback from local actors, or initiate their own research in special cases, to satisfy the same requirement. Through these and other feedback mechanisms, teachers would be able to launch their own research projects and participate on committees for existing projects. Explicit review processes could also be made available, ensuring that teachers actively engage their students and maintain or increase their expertise. We also propose fitting classroom techniques to students who enrol through the regular, non-sorting process, turning the instructor into a kind of empirically backed artisan. This would give teachers more responsibilities, but it would simplify the reform process by introducing fewer structural changes to the existing system.

We recognize that these measures might be seen as a form of monitoring, so we urge that they be implemented in way that made the benefits of participating in research at various levels obvious to all concerned. The existing school system would be deeply involved in every aspect of our proposal; however, only a limited number of practitioners, students, and classrooms would provide research sites, generate ideas, and offer feedback at any one time. Others would operate "normally," except for their ability to take advantage of new research findings.

We have organized the presentation of our proposal for adaptive education in the following way. In Chapter 2, entitled "Foundations for an Evidence-driven Institution," we argue for a greater role for educational research, with specific qualities that we think are crucial to the adaptive education model. We posit an institution designed to be malleable in eliciting and addressing emerging issues, and we propose novel ways to communicate key findings. We also explain the model in relation to the priority it places on salient contextual differences, as well as its local resonance. We demonstrate that findings, while generally communicated as universal in their applicability, also contain enough nuances to be individualistic.

In Chapter 3, we apply the concept of pragmatism as a theory of human action to the institutional scale. We use the theoretical contributions of Roberto Unger and contemporary notions of democratic experimentalism and constant reform to argue for a thoroughly experimental educational institution. The crux of this chapter lies in our rendering the concept of experiment in relation to local issues and connections on the one hand and the latest research techniques and findings on the other.

Chapter 4 continues our redesign efforts with details about the replication of experiments and, eventually, their widespread adoption. We highlight and explain the need to design, systematically but responsively, the research to fit the context. Of particular importance are the criteria for interpreting data and defining success, both of which must be clear and respectful. The chapter also contains guidelines for developing and maintaining projects in the Epistemic Division in an ethical manner. In particular, we are concerned with ensuring that students and other participants are able to opt out of the research project without recourse. In addition, we propose a social contract that would bind partners around the collective effort and the larger institutional goals.

In Chapter 5 we address the key role of teachers in adaptive education. Here our main objective is to examine the kinds of changes that would be necessary to teacher education under the new model, including the focus on inquiry and educational partnerships. We try to clarify both what it means to teach and how the ability to teach is learned. The reader will find these two clarifications are moving targets at a moment when education is under scrutiny at the highest levels.

Chapter 6 provides a thorough description of the Epistemic Division and the departments within it that would generate and maintain a rigorous knowledge base for educational practice. We describe each department completely according to the processes we anticipate transpiring in the life of a research project. We detail the processes involved in eliciting ideas and conducting and disseminating research, using three examples hypothetically to ground the design we put forward.

In the concluding chapter, we summarize the preceding materials and offer next steps.

2 The Foundations of an Evidence-Based Institution

Much of what we cover in this book can be construed as a dispute over inquiry: how it is done, and the constraints that operate upon it. The dispute begins with the scientific method itself. And although we certainly believe in the efficacy of systematic observation with an eye to generalization, where we depart from conventional practice in educational policy, if not in educational research as well, is the reach of our generalizations.

In the Introduction we touched briefly on the problems involved in treating students as comparable units. In short, people learn differently and have different backgrounds that impact on their educational experience. When students are grouped together, we question how successfully teachers distinguish one from another. Teaching to the statistical mean might produce gains in learning for some, but we would prefer not to abandon students who are further from the mean to an educational approach insensitive to their predispositions. At the very least, schools and teachers need to be able to deploy a number of techniques to reach a larger number of students.[1] In the ideal case, we would provide individualized lesson plans.

Perhaps even more to the point, the learning experience is intimately tied to infinitely complex social contexts. Suppose you want to solve a set of math problems with your friends. The way you go about it, and the success of various approaches, will vary according to the number of friends – one, two, or twenty – and to the specific people involved. If you have one friend with exceptional mathematical skills, your best approach probably will be to follow her lead. If the group consists of twenty people with mediocre skills, you might do better to move procedurally, talking things out as you go, and, we hope, not becoming confused in the process. The more granularity we insist on (for example, race, gender, class of participants, time of day, supply of coffee), the more factors and permutations of social context we have to consider. The social context involves, just to start, the school, the residential neighbourhood, family life, time commitments from extra-curricular activities, and biological factors induced by nutrition and exercise.

Despite this complexity, humans do a fairly good job of weeding out irrelevant parts of the situation. It might not matter, for example, whether your math-solving friends are male or female, so you can ignore that factor. This process of narrowing down the relevant char-acteristics of the social context is what allows us to generalize – and, incidentally, is also one of the sources of statistical regularity. When we consider the learning experience in school, we can usually overlook the physical differences between classrooms, for example: some teach-ers might arrange desks in rows and columns, others might use round tables to encourage collaboration. But most jurisdictions have building layouts that are standardized, whether by design or by coincidence, and so most classrooms are rectangular with windows, and very few are circular and windowless. Similarly, if students vary in how effec-tively they learn, it is not the shape of the room that is responsible. But that leaves any number of other, more salient factors to consider, making it hard to know how much we can generalize our findings about these techniques.

Adding to this challenge is that the components of society are con-stantly changing, sometimes slowly, but always by enough to make us worry about the dancing landscape that educators face. What works at one moment might not work in five years' time. Even when we docu-ment relationships between variables in the data, social scientists are careful to treat them tentatively; this is probably truer in the long run than it is in the short term, but the point stands. Our education prac-tices do evolve, but in the past these changes have come in fits and starts, amid periods of stagnation. Would it be better to make regular adjustments over time, rather than reform approaches only once they are obsolete?

It seems a tall order to develop a science of education that is qualified by time, sensitive to differences in the social context, and geared not only towards the statistical mean, but also towards individual students. But the situation is not really all that intractable. Research does, in fact, measure change over time, and often picks out salient contextual differences as well. The problem is one of communication and interpretation. Policy makers, administrators, and teachers are shown "findings" that researchers do not circumscribe enough, lending the results an inappropriate aura of universal application.

Just as these practical problems with advancing a nuanced approach to educational science do not loom quite as large on second glance, so the theoretical challenges are not insurmountable either. We argue that the philosophical tradition of pragmatism offers a way forward. Its theory of inquiry is based on a sophisticated understanding of learning and action, and applies not only to individuals but also to groups and organizations. Pragmatism is no arbitrary choice as a model. It has a long history in education, contributing to pedagogical innovations, playing a pivotal role in the educational efforts of a number of social movements, and spurring on the progressive education movement. We return to this topic in Chapter 3.

An Inquisitive Tendency

For pragmatists such as Charles Peirce and John Dewey, humans possess a fundamental disposition towards inquiry, which explains why it has been rigorously endorsed and developed by institutions as diverse as law and science. Inquiry refers to a move from a position of doubt to one of belief, or to a place where we are warranted to assert certain things about the matter at hand. This is the most typical way of thinking about inquiry: the process through which we gather evidence and evaluate the efficacy of our beliefs and actions.[2] We spend a hefty portion of our lives trying to do just that.

Today we are used to thinking about inquiry as something deliberate. We follow logical principles in order to make justified deductions and form statistical principles that validate inductive reasoning. On top of that, we have developed systematic methodologies that proffer us with procedures to gather and analyse evidence. This is, of course, both helpful and necessary. But Dewey and other pragmatists have argued that we also need to understand the practical grounding of inquiry.[3] We use it every day in simple and implicit ways to guide us through tricky situations. Researchers and others who focus on the principles that underlie the process forget that lay people produce nuanced forms of knowledge as well. This is not to dismiss the importance of deliberate inquiry, only to point out that all forms of inquiry are worth our consideration.

Framing the issue in terms of daily human behaviour means moving away from the strict notion that inquiry is about trying to settle some belief. Instead, we need to think about settling the situation, and to do that we need to consider the pragmatist theory of action. Pragmatism understands human experience as a continuous process of adaptation.[4] Every day presents us with new challenges that force us to adopt new behaviours. These problematic situations stem from the natural and social environments we move through in everyday life. In ecological terms, over time we adapt ourselves to various situations, involving different combinations of actors, institutions, cultural presuppositions, and physical parameters. Just as other living creatures thrive or perish depending on how well they adapt to the environment, so too do humans, although the consequences are not usually so dramatic. For example, students often fail to adapt their attention and work habits to the demands of educational institutions. In the short term, their grades suffer, but the long-term difficulties associated with this maladaptation are no less palpable. They might have trouble adjusting their behaviour once they enter the workforce, which ultimately might deprive them of career advancement and financial remuneration. On the other hand, more relaxed work habits can be adaptable in other ways. They might induce lower levels of stress (and its related health risks) by shielding individuals from certain jobs that place undue tension on work-life balance. Those who do adapt to the demands of higher education might enter high-stress careers that call for adaptive techniques of their own, such as meditation or effective time-management.

When we ask what is being adapted, the only possible response is action. William James put the issue this way: "a man possesses of learning only so much as comes out of him in action, and a monk is a good preacher only so far as his deeds proclaim him such, for every tree is known by its fruits."[5] If we try to adapt to a situation where the primary challenge is physical (for example, there is no door through which to exit a room), the only reasonable response is to involve our physical bodies. It is not possible to think our way out of a room, nor can we physically reconstitute ourselves to address the issue. Instead, we need to make use of an already existing space, such as a window, to make our escape or create a gap ourselves by making a hole. Situations can just as easily involve actions that are primarily cognitive in nature, as when we solve math problems or develop reasonable expectations as part of cognitive behavioural therapy.

Most situations contain several possible modes of action. Imagine the complexities associated with adapting to cultural diversity. Physical bodies have phenotypical differences, making it possible to respond to different races in a violent manner or to arrange physical space to achieve segregation. But racism can be equally founded upon cultural features. The response to these differences, physical or cultural, is invariably bound up with the responder's own cultural identities, emotions, and ways of thinking; thus, people might respond by retreating into individualism, asserting that the contemporary plurality and disagreement among perspectives is irreconcilable, or by enacting a form of epistemic closure, protecting their own beliefs at all costs while suggesting that theirs is the (only) objective truth. The possibilities for action here are nearly infinite. But, in this case, it is more likely that certain forms of actions precede others – violent repression, for instance, is often the result of a prior maladaptive emotional response to perceived threats. In all cases, however, individuals respond according to their understanding of the situation.[6]

Adaptation requires that we develop behavioural tendencies to address specific situations, the effectiveness of which determines success or failure. Pragmatism refers to these tendencies as habits. Consider for a moment that people develop habits for every recurring situation in life. At an early age we develop the cognitive and muscular habits for crawling and walking. Later we incorporate into our habitual repertoire social norms such as writing with pen and paper, using the sidewalk as a pedestrian, and saying "thank you," in part to gain acceptance into the wider community. As students we learn classroom rules such as raising our hand to ask a question. In addition to these complex habits, each person has simple behavioural quirks that are equally habitual.[7]

Many readers will note that some of the habits we refer to are not specific to individual situations. Diversity and penmanship, for example, are part of countless distinct environments. In fact, it is crucial to understand that habits apply to a range of situations. Humans like to reason by analogy. When problems arise *in action*, our intuition tells us to transpose existing habits to the new situation, especially when similarities exist between the respective environments. Even though no two situations are completely alike, attending to the full range of particularities would be paralyzing. Some crossover in habits enables us to ignore the less salient aspects of a situation. Habits are themselves a creative adaptation to the immediate environment, which is invariably slightly different from others that preceded it.[8] Walking or driving might be fully incorporated into our repertoires by the time we are adults, but at each moment there are new objects to avoid, and habits help us do that.

Our habits also vary in their resistance to change for diverse reasons that depend on perspective. From the perspective of the actor, some habits seem more entrenched and harder to replace. Smokers and drug users regularly struggle with addiction, a complicated habit that involves not only decision-making patterns, but complex biochemical dependency and urges as well. People with sedentary lifestyles face the same issue: their habit of inactivity seems especially harder to adjust or overcome than other habits that shape their everyday lives. The perspective of the observer, however, might be quite different. When people in their surroundings resist change, the observer might see the problem as one of commitment, with friends, family, or neighbours stuck in their ways by choice, lack of motivation, or unwillingness to change.

These examples of differing perspectives could easily be reversed because, experientially speaking, both actors and observers can see habits in many ways. We might perceive them as part of our identity, as decision-making tendencies, and even as illnesses. Many actors feel they are too lazy to exercise, too weak to resist temptation, or lack the character to change their habits. Others do not single out their own habits at all: they might tend towards consumerism, but they regard that as part of who they are. Similarly, the observer sometimes treats the other people's bad habits as afflictions or sufferings or even moral failings, rather than as part of their identity.

One issue that arises from the differential entrenchment of habit is characterized by what Dewey called rigid habits,[9] which are the least amenable to change on a mass scale. For social change to be possible, large groups of people need to be willing to part with their habits. They might need to learn to look at the world in different ways, as when social movements and governments fight for equal rights and discrimination protection for marginalized groups. Or they might need to learn something as simple as which waste products can be composted, repurposed, or recycled. But if people develop habits that are resistant to change, these goals become much harder to achieve, and it might take generational turnover for attitudes, knowledge, and behaviour to change. For this reason Dewey thought it was crucial to encourage (and teach) people to have an open mind and never to be too committed to current practices and beliefs. By contrast Unger argues that it is the social situation, not the individual, that determines characteristics such as rigidity and plasticity of behaviour.[10] Despite this difference, Unger wholeheartedly agrees with Dewey that rigid habits limit the potential for social change.

Habits find their shadow in creative action. Although habits represent our capacity for repetitive behaviour, creativity encompasses our ability to adapt.[11] When we encounter situations that frustrate our attempts to respond with habitual behaviour, we are forced to develop new solutions. That is, when our response to a situation becomes unsettled, we embark on a process of inquiry to find a better way of addressing the problem.

Note that habitual behaviour is not *opposed* to creativity, but to reflective behaviour. Creativity is the cognitive device that transforms our habits. Reflection, meanwhile, is a deliberate consideration of possible courses of action that necessarily resists the tendency towards habituation. Imagine that you wake up in your bedroom, only to find that the doorway has been filled with drywall – an April fool's joke courtesy of an angry significant other. Clearly your habit of turning the doorknob to open an exit is no longer feasible. There are various actions you might try instead. You shout, "Honey, this isn't funny!" Perhaps there is no reply, so you try ramming the wall with your shoulder where the doorway used to be, but all you get for your effort is a bruise. Then you realize that your bedroom has a window that lets out into the garden, and thus you make your escape.

Creative action is not immediately converted into habit. Tomorrow, when you wake up, your first instinct will still be to reach for the doorknob. Singular events remain isolated, though they might be lodged in our memory. If, however, you find that the doorway remains replaced with drywall, the adaptive process will continue. You roll your eyes. Maybe you shout, again with no effect. But remembering your bruised shoulder, you walk to the window and hop down into the bed of azaleas. Eventually, a new habit forms: every morning you will get out of bed and walk straight to the bedroom window and climb down the wooden stairs you have placed outside where the azaleas once stood. Not all creative actions become habits over time: some are found wanting, others are helpful only for one-off events. We learn this through inquiry.

Dewey was careful to note that this process of exchange between habit and creativity is continuous.[12] That is, habit is always involved in creativity, and creativity in habit. In the first place, as mentioned above, no two situations are exactly alike. Every application of habit requires some creative adaptation: word selection needs to be different, our balance needs to be adjusted constantly as we move, and our stream of thought necessarily changes as we live our lives. Similarly, many inquiries finish by taking ideas from past experience to address the shortcomings of some habit. Children learn to walk and speak because they watch their parents do so. You knew to use the window because you have either climbed out through one before or have heard of someone else doing the same.

Inquiry is also continuous because settled situations can become unsettled, making current habits obsolete. This is what spurred Dewey's concerns about rigid habits. Because there is no guarantee that the solution we apply to a problem will remain effective, we need to be ready to search for something more appropriate to the changing context. If people (or institutions) refuse to adjust their habits to changing situations, they become less effective.

At this point pragmatism might seem virtually identical to rational choice theory. People go about their lives and make decisions moment by moment to maximize their returns. But pragmatism and rational choice are noticeably different theories of human action. Pragmatists do not believe that people make decisions through reason – most of us do not tally pros and cons or employ some kind of utilitarian calculus in our day-to-day lives. Instead, pragmatism insists that we deploy an experimenting intelligence, inquiring continuously into our changing environment. When you found yourself trapped in the bedroom, you just tried things to see what would happen: you shouted to see if someone would come, you rammed the wall to see if you could open a hole, and finally you tried using the window to exit the room. In the pragmatist account, humans are bound in habit and experimentation, rather than calculation and reason, meaning that we do not always choose maximal behaviour. Ramming the wall seemed like a good idea at the time, not because you had thought the whole thing through (otherwise you would have no bruise!), but because you thought it might work. Had you been of a clearer mind, would you have done the same? Emotions might cloud our judgment, but the conclusions we arrive at through deliberation are no less tentative.[13] We literally think through our options, playing them out in our minds, where the consequences are less real.

Solving Problems Together

If you are impatient, you might be wondering why it matters how individuals approach inquiry. After all, we are concerned here with institutions, and institutions are about aggregating, organizing, and disseminating information, not about how regular people go about making decisions. The issue is this: institutions and other organizations do not think, let alone solve problems, except through their members. There are two parts to this notion. First, as Dewey emphasized,[14] people develop habits within a social context: being in an organization opens up particular kinds of habit-formation processes for workers and passers-through alike. Second, and of more concern here, many of the mechanisms that apply to individuals also apply to groups.

As with individuals, groups of people can recognize when they are being affected by the consequences of some action. This recognition can even provide the impetus for acknowledging the existence of a *we*. Say, for example, teachers go on strike. Beforehand there might have been a loose notion among students that they are a group, but the recognition that striking teachers might jeopardize their chance of gaining entrance to a post-secondary institution or even of graduating might galvanize students according to their shared difficulties. Dewey believed this was how the public constitutes itself as a political entity:[15] once there is self-awareness in the group, its members can start experimenting with a response, directed not towards controlling the situation, but towards protecting the collective from the consequences that impinge upon it. This might mean restricting relevant activities through the law and other institutions, or minimizing the impact of the consequences.[16]

Putting these kinds of responses together in the real world, however, can be complicated.[17] The simplest solution – and, incidentally, the one most mainstream economists deploy – is to add everything together. Ten people in room equals ten different collections of skills, knowledge, and experience, or ten different parts of an answer. Put them together, and you might happen upon something special. By contrast, Dewey and Mary Parker Follett argued that collective inquiry is carried forward not just by pooling experiences, but also through dialogue. New ideas for solving emergent issues do not develop on their own. Instead, they intermingle with other ideas, bouncing back and forth between participants and incorporating corrections when the need arises. In this way, ideas improve through deliberation as well as through experimentation.[18]

Consider how this differs from current approaches to problem solving in groups. The most common approach looks at the individuals in a group and sees a diversity of perspectives. Assuming that some perspectives are better than others at solving particular problems, the more diverse the group – at least in terms of perspectives – the more likely the group will hit upon a successful way to address the problem. We can certainly fit adaptive functions into this rubric – brainstorming sessions, for instance, usually involve some dialogue in addition to a diversity of ideas – but there is no requirement to do so. This way of thinking simply assumes that the more perspectives there are on a topic, the more likely a solution will be found – which is the logic that underwrites crowdsourcing.[19] Once we factor in the interactional dynamics that affect the way we share and develop ideas, these insights become less straightforward. Too many people in the room (say, in Parliament or Congress) can make it hard to trade and refine ideas, even if their combined perspectives would suggest effective ways forward. To develop an idea dialogically, everyone needs to be able to participate fully and equitably.

Another contemporary approach to problem solving in groups is a little less intuitive. It turns out that the average opinion of a crowd of people can be rather on point, and in many cases is more accurate than the opinion of any single person in the crowd.[20] In effect, we can solve problems together without even working together. This is a boon for news outlets wanting to pick out the most important news stories, or for people trying to sort through first-hand accounts of how big or how heavy an ox is. However, most of our challenges are more complex. Point estimates might aggregate well, but elaborate action schemes do not. These require more give and take, and more experimentation to get right.

In contrast to these approaches, pragmatism grounds its dialogical method of shared inquiry in the adaptive element in human experience. Each of us, as participant and witness, has special knowledge about the situations we move through on a daily basis, in addition to our understanding of the expectations that go along with our social roles.[21] This knowledge arises from the habit-forming process that allows us to streamline decision making.[22] As we saw above, instead of reconsidering repetitive situations with each successive appearance, we make use of standard responses based on previously successful courses of action. Over time our experiences, trading on our acquaintances and even our own linguistic capabilities, per Dewey, reveal pitfalls and minor details in how we apply our habits, forcing us to adjust in the process.[23] Through this continuous process, we are able to gain an awareness of the relevant nuances contained in our daily circumstances.

We argue that collaboration begins when local actors become aware of consequences that bear on their shared experiences. Elementary school staff, for example, might insist on locking the school doors at 4 p.m. to all students, only to discover that three children from low-income homes rely on a 4:20 bus to get home. Instead of forcing them to wait alone down the street, staff might revise their stance. Over time, however, several parents who had previously made efforts to collect their children on time might begin to take advantage of the new policy by treating the school like an extended daycare service. This makes it apparent to the staff that they need to return to closing the school doors at 4 p.m., but with exceptions made on the basis of parental request or staff discretion. The involvement of staff in their immediate situation makes it possible for them to recognize relevant details that might go unnoticed by policy makers removed from the environment.

In this example, it takes little more than simple awareness to make room for exceptions to the school's policy. As Follett pointed out, there is nothing especially group-like when everyone agrees from the get go.[24] Imagine instead that no public or school buses serve this school, that some students live too far away to walk home, that their parents cannot pick them up until 6 p.m., well after staff have gone home, and that no other parents are able to give them a ride. Now the problem is less trivial. Organizing an after-school program is probably ideal, but one teacher will point out that someone has to put in the work. Should teachers do this on their own time? Should the school hire outside assistance? Eventually someone might indicate that there is no room in the budget for an after-school program. With this the idea takes on new shape, as it needs to be brought to the school district. Local knowledge makes it clear that something needs to be done, and even provides a possible solution, but without the support of a larger institution the idea might fall on its face. In the meantime one teacher suggests that they find volunteers to put something on after school, perhaps rotating among different teachers and parents so that no one is overburdened. It also might be proposed that existing after-school clubs be approached to see if they would be willing to organize something at school. What might emerge in the end is a time-sharing solution (at least until the school district finds a more sustainable solution) whereby on some nights the local youth basketball league keeps the gym open for training and scrimmage, and on other nights parent or teacher volunteers provide some kind of program.

Dialogue adds value over and above the pooling of perspectives by letting ideas grow through their contact with one another. The process moves beyond just picking out the best idea; the ideas produced through dialogue are often superior to any single perspective, simply because group-generated ideas can adopt the best bits of each idea to become a composite. Of course, it is not so easy to succeed at dialogue in real life. There is an element of dialogue at the core of how we learn to be human, as Mead noted.[25] Our sense of self comes in part from our perception of how other people see and respond to us. But deliberate discussions in a group require the commitment and full participation of every member; people need to be willing to hear an idea and to add something to it, setting aside partisan divides and other squabbles.

This all works best in smaller groups. Five or six teachers are likely to find a cooperative solution to a local problem in a way that four thousand teachers cannot.[26] Once we start looking at big groups, deliberate communication becomes hard to maintain. This is doubly significant in an era of mass communication and imagined communities, since the practicalities that facilitate dialogue break down. Commenting on the demise of the public as a political force for these very reasons, Dewey suggested that we have not yet adjusted our practices with new realities in mind. In his words, nearly a century ago, "We have inherited, in short, local town-meeting practices and ideas. But we live and act and have our being in a continental national state. We are held together by non-political bonds and the political forms are stretched and legal institutions patched in an *ad hoc* and improvised manner to do the work they have to do."[27] The same holds true for education, and so we come to the crucial question for educators who are committed to an empirical approach: How do we organize inquiry with the modern condition in mind without abandoning local knowledge and dialogue? Our solution is rooted in the pragmatist revival in political science, driven largely by Roberto Unger. We argue that, instead of using the educational institution as a hierarchical bureaucracy, it should be reconfigured as a mediating device between localities, where techniques can be developed and tested as part of a thoroughly experimental institution – the topic of the next chapter.

3   The Search for a Blueprint

In the previous chapter, we saw that the pragmatist view of inquiry is all-encompassing, including not only the scientific enterprise but also everyday problem solving. It should come as no surprise, then, that a number of pragmatists, inspired by advancements in the understanding of human psychology, have tried to reform public institutions such as education and government by putting the practice of inquiry at their core. What should startle you, however, is how unsuccessful these efforts have been. Until Roberto Unger wrote *False Necessity* in the late 1980s or, if you prefer, until Michael Dorf and Charles Sabel crafted their hefty article, "A Constitution of Democratic Experimentalism" ten years later, there was no blueprint for what an inquiry-based institution should look like, at least from a pragmatist perspective.[1] Earlier writers such as John Dewey, whether because they were good scholars or bad activists, seem to have left the reform movement to figure out the specifics on its own.

That being said, early pragmatists went out of their way to find new uses of inquiry to solve old institutional problems. Consider the challenge of establishing a scientific form of education. To test his theories about learning and human nature, Dewey founded a laboratory school at the University of Chicago. When it opened in 1896, the public, much as it does today, widely disapproved of the school system. The philosopher was hoping to offer an alternative that could encourage better learning and ultimately facilitate a more vibrant participatory democracy. Building on his own work, Dewey designed a two-part structure to the program. Students, who ranged from four to sixteen years of age, were allowed to explore, capitalizing on their natural inclination towards inquiry and mastering course content along the way.

Teachers were tasked with the responsibility of designing experiences that would inculcate desired content, and of implementing the curriculum in a way that captured the interest of students. In part because of its success, but also because of Dewey's reputation as a scholar, the laboratory school at Chicago was quickly heralded as the best of its kind and as signalling a new approach to education.[2]

Others of its kind followed, and today laboratory schools (or demonstration schools, as they are sometimes called) are centres for education research at their respective institutions, often focusing on one particular school of thought. The School at Columbia University, for instance, has adopted the perspective of knowledge-based constructivism, while others, such as the University of Toronto Schools, choose not to work from a single theoretical background. Whatever the case, faculty design the curriculum and classroom experience to test hypotheses with ready-made samples and high academic standards. In the long run this allows education researchers to improve curriculum, teaching standards, and pedagogical technique.

Over time these institutions have taken on new aspects, including teacher training, which is increasingly common at laboratory schools. Given the opportunity to hone their craft in idealized circumstances, student educators teach lessons under observation by mentors who can offer feedback. (Some laboratory schools have been designed with rooms that overlook, or are adjacent to, the classroom to facilitate observation. Today there is little need for anything but video camera equipment.) The main attraction of this practice is the controlled environment: students who gain admission tend to excel academically, suffer fewer behavioural problems, and can be selected according to training needs. But these schools also create something of an artificial atmosphere, as the conditions rarely simulate real life and the participants are always aware that they might be under observation.

The prohibitive cost of running laboratory schools, however, has limited their number, so the significance of this pragmatist contribution might be lost on many people. But laboratory schools embody the ideals of the scientific approach to education. It was not enough for figures such as Dewey to expound theories of learning and education; theories need to be tested if anyone is to derive benefit from them.

These same ideals launched the progressive education movement. In the late nineteenth and early twentieth centuries, education was largely designed to prepare the student for university. This entailed rote memorization of abstract knowledge and the study of classical philosophy and literature, which formed the core curriculum. Not surprisingly, in the United States, where compulsory education had not yet taken hold, working-class families saw little reason to send their children to school if they were unlikely to attend university. Emerging to address this underlying problem of inequity, the progressive education movement hoped to establish pedagogical and curricular principles on the basis of solid scientific evidence. It argued persuasively that people learn best through experience and that project-based teaching would serve students of all class conditions better than the prevailing system. Underlying its approach was a firm belief that education should tailor itself to the child, rather than the reverse.

The architect of the progressive education movement's beliefs was William Heard Kilpatrick, whose mentor in graduate school was none other than John Dewey. Kilpatrick would go on to be a collaborator and colleague of Dewey's for many years, a partnership that culminated in their leadership of the progressive education movement. Kilpatrick also penned one of the seminal works in the philosophy of education.[3]

An early adopter of community service learning techniques, the progressive education movement has carved out a legacy that extends beyond its status as an alternative to contemporary national school systems. Especially during the Great Depression, it helped provide educational opportunities to children who otherwise would have been caught up in economic necessity. Although progressive ideas came under general suspicion during the Cold War, leading to an eventual decline in their importance, the movement persists in various forms today, most recently in its opposition to the No Child Left Behind policy in the United States. Nonetheless, its advocates have never proposed concrete changes to the institution itself, choosing instead to focus on practice.

The exception to this trend was Mary Parker Follett, who proposed that institutions be based on a series of nested groups. In the business sector this concept began with work teams, and Follett quickly became influential for her positions on leadership and teamwork. It is mainly her writing on democracy, however, that reverberates with us. Follett argued that governments need to start from the ground up, because true democracy is based on deliberation and dialogue.[4] Her argument rests on a unique conception of inquiry (or problem solving, if you prefer) in what she called the "group process." The main benefit of groups (as opposed to crowds or mobs, both of which operate on the basis of influence and contagion) is that, in such a forum, people may talk through and develop their ideas. Individuals bring their own thoughts to the table, to be sure, but as they start sharing their knowledge and experience, these ideas take on an entirely new flavour. Follett believed that they become group ideas, belonging not to any one person, but simultaneously produced by each participant. Solutions intermingle to produce responses more effective than any single idea.[5]

This kind of cooperation can exist only within certain kinds of groups, according to Follett. People need to be willing to relinquish control of their ideas and to be full participants in the ongoing discussion. That is why small groups – in which regular face-to-face interactions happen in daily life – work best. She considered neighbourhoods – which she saw as featuring a high level of civility and fair-mindedness – the best example of small-group cooperation.

Using neighbourhoods as a starting point, Follett devised a novel structure for government in which neighbourhood groups would try to wrangle with affairs particular to their situation. Larger regional groups – neighbourhoods of neighbourhoods, if you will – would meet to discuss matters with a bit more generality, and so on. In this way, the institution would build layer upon layer until it reached national and international size and deal with issues that affect everyone. Each level would borrow ideas from lower and higher levels, as group representatives moved up and down the institutional ladder for various meetings.

In the end, however, Follett entertained a few too many unrealistic assumptions. Although the group process sometimes might produce superior ideas, at other times the ideal response might come from a single expert, and talking about it and modifying it through dialogue might only dilute it. More problematic was the premise that groups form more or less organically. For the group process to work, people need to be familiar with each other and be willing to work together. The higher order the group, the less tenable this premise becomes. How do different neighbourhoods become familiar with one another or form working relationships? How do groups of neighbourhoods do the same at the next level? Follett never answered these questions satisfactorily: she thought that public lectures might foster solidarity and mutual understanding across a region, but that was virtually all she had to say. Recent findings even cast doubt on her basic premise that neighbourhoods are friendly and cooperative places.[6]

Even though some of Follett's assumptions were unfounded, contemporaneous and later experiments in social organization successfully

developed and deployed similar ideas in more limited arenas. Hull
House, established in Chicago by Jane Addams, was among the first
settlement houses in the United States. It was a project in which the
middle and upper classes lived in community with the poor. The live-
in volunteers organized activities designed to alleviate the problems of
the neighbourhood, sharing knowledge with neighbours, and even
providing them with jobs through cooperative projects, such as a book-
bindery business that was housed in the building for a time. It was, in
this way, an experiment in adaptation to the urban environment. Its
stated objective was to live cooperatively and to engage in egalitar-
ian relations (or "democratic relations") across class lines. Hull House
also made itself available to organized groups that needed a space in
which to gather, and served as a meeting point for activists addressing
women's suffrage and workers' rights. More than other adult education programs that hoped to encourage grassroots social change,
Hull House focused on bringing the residents of a single community
together to address its problems, rather than explicitly bringing diverse
communities together to learn from one another.

Hull House quickly became one of the adult education movement's
most influential centres, serving as an example of effective practice in
reducing urban poverty. Its programs were rooted in pragmatist ideas –
unsurprising, given the importance of pragmatism to the development
of adult education in North America. It emphasized hands-on learning
with relevance to everyday life, and addressed everything from sewing
and literacy to money management and union organizing. Addams
herself was responsible for many of these programs.

At this point the relationship of Hull House to pragmatism becomes
more explicit. Because of its location in Chicago, one of the earliest proponents of Hull House was John Dewey. Already occupied with his
laboratory school only a few miles away at the University of Chicago,
he was thrilled to find in Addams someone with similar intentions.
Together they worked to refine his theories and their respective programs. Dewey visited Hull House on numerous occasions, becoming
a collaborator in the programs and a friend of several activists sta-
tioned there. The urban focus of the settlement house did not go unnoticed in the wider university community. Addams was contracted by
the University of Chicago's Department of Sociology to be a lecturer,
and would go on to collaborate with several members of the department. At the time the so-called first Chicago School of sociology was in
full bloom, reinvigorating the field with its detailed ethnographies of

urban life by figures such as Robert Park. The connection here should not be overlooked. After Dewey, pragmatism was largely institutionalized in sociology through the University of Chicago. Indeed, symbolic interactionism – one of the dominant schools of thought in the contemporary social sciences, and developed by University of Chicago sociologists – is in many ways the systematized and operationalized form of pragmatism. Today Jane Addams is generally considered a pragmatist philosopher in her own right.[7]

A similar entity to Hull House is the Highlander Folk School in Tennessee, which ventures to improve social conditions through adult education. Its pedagogy begins and ends with the life experiences of real people, and focuses on social problems that are encountered in everyday life, from persistent racism to struggles to achieve equitable working conditions to the threat of job loss because of economic conditions or new technologies. Like Hull House, Highlander operates based on its own pragmatism-inspired workshop model.[8] But rather than establishing firm neighbourhood roots, it acts as an activist training ground.

The origins of the pragmatist practices employed at Highlander lie in the intellectual development of its founder, Myles Horton. Interested from his youth in establishing an adult education program to help the people of rural Tennessee, Horton moved to New York to study the social gospel under noted theologian Reinhold Niebuhr. The latter is especially important in theology for developing the view of Christian Realism, partly on the basis of the psychology of William James. Interestingly, despite being thoroughly influenced by pragmatism, Niebuhr was a constant opponent of Dewey's irreligious views in the mass media. Horton was deeply influenced by his mentor, and adopted many of Niebuhr's views as his own for the remainder of his life.

Recognizing that Horton's interests extended far beyond theology, Niebuhr recommended that Horton move to Chicago to study under Robert Park in the University of Chicago's blossoming Department of Sociology, where, incidentally, Jane Addams was then teaching. Given his interest in poverty, Horton took quickly to the research on urban sociology. At some point Park mentioned that Danish folk schools operated on premises similar to Horton's own ideas, which prompted Horton to visit that country and later to combine some of the practices he witnessed there with those he had learned from his pragmatist mentors.

Highlander typically organizes workshops when activists or citizens who are encountering systemic problems in their local environments approach it. (Its leaders are emphatically against diagnosing social issues themselves. Instead, they emphasize the need to trust the experiences of locals who encounter challenges first-hand.) The workshops bring together a diverse set of people to talk about common problems in order to address them in a cooperative way. Diversity within the group is seen to be especially important, since it allows participants to learn from different points of view, to develop a comprehensive understanding of the problem, and to address it more effectively. Instead of taking up a problem and experimenting in the material world, participants use their own past experiences as experiments in themselves. The workshop model effectively multiplies life experiences, increasing the potential for solutions.

Highlander became well known during the civil rights era for hosting integrated discussion groups that addressed racial segregation in schools, public institutions, and urban ghettos. The story of how the citizenship schools were created through Highlander's involvement is illustrative of the problem-based learning by monitoring that characterizes its methodology. At the time, many Southern states enforced specific provisions of Jim Crow laws to suppress black voting. Perhaps most infamously, they administered literacy tests to the largely uneducated black community as a ploy to refuse voter registration to large numbers of people.

Esau Jenkins was the quintessential local leader. He drove the late-night bus, was an assistant pastor, and headed a handful of community organizations in the town of John's Island, South Carolina. He also regularly encountered the challenges of segregated schools and political disenfranchisement. Jenkins became convinced that the biggest problem facing John's Island was the rampant illiteracy that kept residents from being registered to vote. As a result of his community involvement, Jenkins attended a Highlander workshop on equality inspired by the United Nations Universal Declaration of Human Rights. The discussions, premised upon the experiences that Jenkins shared with the group, revealed that literacy testing was the single most important factor preventing black people from voting in every region represented at the workshop. A working group comprised of Jenkins, Septima Clark, and Bernice Robinson returned to John's Island to found an educational institute designed to give black residents the literacy skills necessary to activate their right to vote. The citizenship schools, as they were called, employed many of the same pragmatist-inspired practices as Highlander used, such as collaboration, life experience, and practical challenges. After an extremely successful early run, the operation of the schools was turned over to Martin Luther King, Jr. and his associates, who founded hundreds more around the United States.

Contemporary Pragmatism

It was not until the late 1980s that a model emerged that looked to local actors for input that could be generalized at a higher institutional level. Paving the way was Roberto Unger, although he approached the matter from a different direction than had the pragmatists who preceded him.[9] His driving concern was to find a way to give ordinary people more control over the social structures – whether political or economic – that control their lives. Pragmatism provided him with a proto-theory of human action, although he did not fully incorporate the actions of the average citizen into his plans for democratic reform.

The governmental structure he proposed relies on grassroots experiments to inform future reforms: localities would generate and apply new ideas, then share their results with one another and with the central institution. But this would still be a *central* institution, with the vast majority of individuals looking in from the outside, except when their experiments were channelled upward to generate reforms. For the most part, Unger proposed an experimenting local government (one that experiments with its policies) tied hierarchically to other levels of government. To skirt the problems of parliamentary gridlock, the powers of each level would be expanded, and their purviews overlapped to provide checks and balances. To keep things moving, a new branch of government would mediate disputes at lower levels of the hierarchy, and take matters to a public referendum if no solution emerged from dialogue.

Despite the model's limitations, Unger took a huge leap towards conceiving what we call an adaptive institution. He suggested that policies, and their structures, need not apply everywhere and for all time, recognizing that human creations are bound by their historical context. At the same time, politics has been crippled by the inability to establish consensus. Since there is no absolute foundation for truth – a recognition that in Unger's opinion sets off the modern era – there will always be disagreement about how best to proceed. We need to foster an environment in which people feel free to disagree and are willing to accept the application of opposing policies. To support such an environment, Unger argued, governments need to generate multiple lines of inquiry in order to respond to diverse situations and satisfy irremediable disputes.

Unger also recognized that a permanent state of change is not viable. Institutions need to be capable of reform and practices adjusted, but moments of stability are also needed, if only to allow improved routines and habits to develop. With that in mind, Unger proposed the idea of mini-constitutions, which would be binding over a limited sphere of action for a limited period of time. They would provide bureaucracy with its mandate as well as its *modus operandi*. We discuss mini-constitutions in more detail in the next chapter when we present the idea of customizable standards.

Gone are Dewey's wait-and-see and Follett's idealism. Their ideas inspired political scientists and policy makers, but they fall short when applied to educational institutions. Unger's goes farther, but his interest lies more in developing experimental government forms than in uncovering spatially and temporally contingent best practices through inquiry. We move farther still with the democratic experimentalism of Michael Dorf and Charles Sabel.

Dorf and Sabel build on Unger's platform by aiming their experimentation towards policy and practice. They propose an experimenting form of democratic governance designed to let citizens use local knowledge to find solutions to fit their particular circumstances.[10] This small-scale experimentation would be tied together by coordinating bodies that require people to share their knowledge with others facing similar challenges. In democratic experimentalism, governance councils would be elected at the local, state, and national levels to determine goals for policy and to evaluate the success of policy implementations – experimental and otherwise – at achieving these goals. Governance councils, in short, would be mediators of public inquiry, and offer a kind of scientific approach to governance. The actual research would be outsourced to firms that presumably would win a bid for the contract. They would coordinate with local citizens to identify needs, along with the relevant conditions in the area, and help put in place their recommendations along the way. Citizens would be at least partially involved in the inquiry, by electing the councils that would represent their interests and guide policy changes and by forcing the research firms to deal with them. Democratic experimentalism, however, would not build on the inquiring faculties in every human being. Inquiry would be accountable to the citizenry, but citizens would not conduct their own experiments. Later on, we show how both can be done in the context of education.

The democratic experimentalism model is not entirely dissimilar from collaborative adaptive management techniques that have been applied in places such as the Glen Canyon Dam in Arizona, where the US Department of the Interior brought together stakeholders to discuss innovative ways to implement procedures to accomplish a number of conflicting goals. At Glen Canyon, the main tension is between the desire to generate electricity and the welfare of the ecology downstream from the dam: environmentalists urge periodic controlled floods to help sustain wildlife in the area, but this practice reduces electric output for the generator. Experiments in water flow under the Glen Canyon Dam Adaptive Management Program have significantly advanced understanding of the relationship between water flow and sedimentation, with important consequences for ecology,[11] but the US government's half-hearted efforts to take this research into account have made it difficult to establish understanding among the stakeholders, and the local environment remains in a tenuous position.[12]

Dorf and Sabel point out that institutions need a way to compare situations if they are to learn from them. If we learn that it is a waste of time and money to enforce laws about dog leashes in a small outer metropolitan suburb in California, where do we apply this bit of knowledge? Can we use it in Philadelphia? What about in rural Nebraska? In democratic experimentalism, administrative agencies would help to determine what conditions and locations are comparable and along what dimensions. Dorf and Sabel reason that these agencies would have the necessary analytical strengths and wide-ranging involvement to take on this task. Presumably, in our dog leash example, we could set narrow limits by saying the finding is at least potentially applicable in other small outer metropolitan suburbs with demographic, cultural, and institutional characteristics similar to the one in California. But this would be overly cautious. It is more likely that some salient features of the dog leash law are either inconsequential or difficult to enforce. Administrative agencies would pick up on this, and forward the findings to other municipalities whose laws share these specific features.

In the same way, this kind of benchmarking helps establish standards that governments can enforce. That is, people have to meet the performance levels set by best practices, whether they are in the midst of an experiment or not. Because the policy field is constantly adjusting to new developments and changing social environments, benchmarking takes on the form of rolling best practices – temporary rules for what works best according to our current knowledge in particular situations. (This is more or less the equivalent of Unger's mini-constitutions.) Benchmarking periodically updates these standards to incorporate improvements gleaned from recent experiments, helping to increase minimum levels of attainment while simultaneously increasing the potential for further improvements.

At least in principle, Dorf and Sabel recognize that many routes can lead to the same end. When governance councils decide how to address a given situation, the best-practice standard should not bind them to a particular method; if they could achieve the same level of success with another solution, they should be welcome to apply it, especially since variety contributes to the inquiry process. We can tolerate a certain level of diversity because, in the end, the various methods would converge in attaining the minimum levels set by rolling best practices.

We should note that, although democratic experimentalism serves as a major inspiration for what follows (along with Unger's institution of constant reform), it comes with its own drawbacks when applied to education. At its worst, benchmarking can help entrench existing best practices when they should be subject to change based on new evidence.[13] Part of the problem is that benchmarking demands that experiments show early positive results. Current best practices might be based on decades of thought backed by extensive research; this body of data commits us to what Thomas Kuhn called "normal science": inquiry designed to bring incremental improvements to existing knowledge.[14] But if research is confined to developing old ideas, what has been becomes the harbinger of what will be, leaving little room for trailblazing. The discovery of genuinely innovative ideas requires both time and a tolerance for failure along the way.

Dorf and Sabel also deploy a fairly rigid notion of experimentation (Unger is more lenient, although his institution is less refined), one that we depart from in dramatic fashion in the next chapter. Following in the tradition established by Donald Campbell,[15] Dorf and Sabel view the experiment with random assignment and control groups as the gold standard, and often as the only appropriate method, for policy research. The trouble with this requirement – beside the fact that a huge amount of social scientific research today would not pass muster – is that it is almost impossible to have truly random assignment in the real world. Even control groups can be hard to arrange. We assert that, although randomness and control groups matter, all evidence counts – it just counts differently in different cases.

The Possibility of Constant Reform

Countless pieces of legislation have been directed towards education reform over the past two centuries, and although the underlying structures of education have not been transformed, change has taken place. To understand the dynamics of the process of transformation, we need to differentiate between two types of modifications that can be made to an institution: those that work to refine operations within an already existing model, and those that adjust the model itself.

Institutions need to adapt to their surroundings, fitting in with related institutions and functioning cohesively within the beliefs and routines of the population. Without these adaptations, an institution can become obsolete, failing to fill its role in society and simultaneously confounding and frustrating the people it is meant to serve. To balance these forces both for and against change, an institution moves through periods of stability and instability, each of which is conducive to different kinds of reform. When the institution is well adjusted to its situation, the need for change is less pronounced and policy makers are less inclined to propose sweeping legislation. Instead, this is a time for fine-tuning its various moving parts to maximize efficiency. If the institution fails to align itself with the structures and people around it, however, dramatic reform becomes more likely. We might still see incremental improvements during such times, but the tension between the status quo and public expectations can also give local and national jurisdictions reason to take risks in pursuing radically creative modifications.

Chris Argyris and Donald Schön address this point in the organizational learning literature. They outline how the cultural assumptions of a workplace, embodied explicitly in rules and regulations and implicitly in the minds of individual persons, can undermine an institution's capacity to recognize shortcomings and adjust quickly in response.[16] For instance, when instructors are assigned to teach an underperforming group of students, there are incentives to inflate test scores artificially if they feel their superiors will blame them for the poor results. Entire schools and districts can operate in similar ways: they might withhold critical information (both positive and negative) to gain status or competitive advantage in the region.

To account for this tendency to ignore underlying assumptions, Argyris and Schön distinguish between "single-loop" and "double-loop" learning. In single-loop learning, institutions address system errors without calling into question their own cultural presuppositions. For example, in the scenario above, administrators might respond by chastising the teachers involved for falsely representing the academic performance of their students. Although this response might solve the immediate problem, it does not address the underlying cause, leaving open the possibility of recurrence. By contrast, in double-loop learning, system leaders evaluate whether their underlying assumptions contribute to the production of system errors, hoping to identify the root trouble. In this case the culture of performance that pervades the teaching profession, perhaps encouraged by tying compensation and promotion to test scores, initiated the conditions that led to the misconduct. Double-loop learning involves finding new ways to motivate teachers without setting up the promotion of grade inflation.

The concepts of single-loop and double-loop learning help us understand the value of structural transformation. That is, when viewed as a system, reforms that leave the design model intact sometimes fail to address the root causes of the malfunction, whereas purposeful adjustments to the institutional structure can address the error and prevent its recurrence. But structural transformation at any level takes place only during times of active policy development, leaving us to ask: Why do institutions go through periods of stagnation and inaction, when policy makers ignore double-loop learning and implement only piecemeal changes? The reason is that, although institutions adapt themselves both to other institutions and to embedded habits and beliefs, they become entrenched in various ways.[17] They develop resistance to major change because the possibilities for reform are constrained by the adaptive relationship they have with their environment. Thus, legislation for reform needs to fit with the institutional relationships, habits, and beliefs that are already taken into account in the existing institutional scheme. One cannot simply push forward with double-loop learning and replace one structure with another. The replacement needs to maintain the functional shape of the original.

Consider this example from product design and technology management. The marketplace is often littered by normative standards based on consumer allegiance, rather than on product superiority.[18] Over time any company hoping to compete for a sizable market share needs to follow these design standards. Imagine trying to release a new math textbook that teaches arithmetic through algebra. Perhaps, over time, research will show conclusively that students gain a better handle on algebra when they start it at an early age, and that their arithmetic skills do not suffer. But it would be exceedingly difficult to find customers for such a book. School systems would brand it unusable with the extant curriculum. Tutors and well-meaning parents would also disregard it because students are evaluated on their ability to master the established curriculum, not on their long-term ability to master the subject. In the same way, policy makers cannot change the education system to eliminate credentials or remove age-based divisions. The possibilities for reform are limited by historical circumstance.

We might also compare the episodic nature of institutional reform with paradigm shifts in science. Kuhn showed, amid considerable controversy and with warranted revisions, that scientific knowledge progresses through alternating stages of normal and revolutionary science.[19] When there is an established set of assumptions within a given explanatory framework, scientists work mainly towards accumulating detail and fleshing out their theoretical trappings. Normal science is, in essence, an effort in puzzle solving. But as problems accumulate that are not easily solved, scientists begin questioning the assumptions that make up the dominant explanatory framework, and revolutionary science begins. Although there is meaning in the distinction, these two stages should not be sharply differentiated,

The comparison here is not perfect. Science is committed to accumulating knowledge, while institutions are tasked with managing complex constellations of behaviour. But the similarities merit at least superficial consideration. The structural transformation of institutions is contingent upon the cumulative effect of challenging puzzles brought on by maladaptation to the environment, and policy makers are certainly compelled to solve problems without incurring the high costs associated with sweeping reform. It seems reasonable to suggest, then, that to some degree the assumptions underlying an institution need to be questioned before double-loop learning can take place or structures transformed.

The complete explanation for periods of institutional stability and instability involves a combination of three factors: double-loop versus single-loop learning, public expectations produced over time, and willingness to question underlying assumptions. Double-loop learning is limited by both public expectations and the ability to solve problems without questioning underlying assumptions. In an interesting twist, this latter point suggests that an institution's double-loop learning is limited by the success of its single-loop learning.

Turning to two of the most prominent debates in education reform – teacher quality and the length of the school day – we get a sense of the way in which many contemporary proposals leave the dominant model intact, opting instead for incremental revisions. As a case in point, the debate about class size is often presented as way to affect teaching quality. Larger class sizes, it is argued, mean that teachers are forced to dilute their attention, causing an overall decline in their effectiveness for each student. Note, however, that reducing class size would leave the larger structure unaffected save for an increase in the total number of classes. Most typical approaches to raising teacher quality follow the same pattern. For example, many people have suggested that teachers need better training programs and that minimum certification requirements should be raised, but in the broader institutional scheme, such changes would serve only to increase the performance of the various specialists employed on the assembly line.

Similarly, discussions around lengthening the school day are limited to changes to the existing system. The assumption underlying these proposals – whether to add another hour in class or to increase tutoring services outside school – is that the basic learning processes in education are effective: since knowledge and learning are cumulative, educational output can be increased by extending the time students spend studying. These reforms are often inspired by comparisons to other countries with similar school systems, and resemble the kind of incremental changes that de facto standards undergo in the marketplace.

The recent interest in school choice provides an interesting, though lonely, counterpoint to the preceding examples because it is an explicit attempt to transform the structural foundations of public education. By creating an education market among primary and secondary schools, either by privatizing the industry or by instituting school choice within the public institution, reformers believe that economic forces of competition would take over, forcing schools to increase quality or risk losing students to other, better-performing schools. Although this is not the approach we take, it is nonetheless an interesting attempt to modify the principles that guide education today.

This discussion raises an interesting question: Can we create social situations (and institutions) that are constantly open to transformative change? Such openness would allow organizations to avoid systematic errors and undertake double-loop learning with regularity. They could adapt more quickly to new information and their changing environments, and avoid the lag caused by periods of stagnation. They could also make sustained progress in attenuating problems such as poverty and manmade climate change by weakening the habits that contribute to them.

Roberto Unger offers the most promising response in *False Necessity*, his massive work of political philosophy.[20] He argues that social environments become entrenched to varying degrees as they become more resistant to the conflicts that emerge in everyday routines, and that differing institutions and belief systems can coexist only when they allow similar levels of freedom to actors. Entrenchment makes it hard to negotiate changes to the environment. The latter point, as we have seen, is one of the limiting factors in reform efforts, as modifications can flounder if they step too far outside the norms of the institutional and ideological context. But here Unger is careful to note that stability does not entail rigidity. An institution can be both stable and flexible. Disentrenchment implies, in its varying degrees, that the context can be adjusted through normal activities, and that people are able to act outside of role and hierarchical structures. We might say, then, that constant reform is the state in which actors are less bound by norms and are empowered freely to develop habits adapted to their purposes in evolving social contexts.

Although his main interests lie in the political system, Unger offers internal justifications for his institutional arrangement that are informative for our purposes. He argues that his revisions would prevent majorities from imposing their will on the rest of the population, present a clearer image of society as the collective project of many people, and make it easier to accomplish the political programs of conservatives and liberals alike. The first two of these justifications are only tangential to this book, but the third has special relevance for us. Education has long struggled to balance its potential for social impact and the need for political neutrality. If, through constant reform, we can provide a platform for educational projects that fall across the political spectrum and expose them to empirical analysis, the institution finally might be able to maintain its neutrality while still making a positive social impact.

Our proposal for adaptive education does not necessarily promote a more activist educational system, but it does use Unger's idea of disentrenchment in its construction of an Epistemic Division for education and its development of new professional norms. Teachers, administrators, students, and community members would all be able to participate in continually establishing new routines suited to the needs of particular situations. In this sense, it aims to engender constant reform.

4 Designing an Inquiring Institution

Now that we have a solid footing in pragmatism (and its numerous forms and disagreements), it is time to move on to something more concrete. How can we create an evidence- and inquiry-based educational institution that takes local experience seriously while still aiming for generalizable (though thoroughly historicized) sets of best practices? We begin this chapter with an examination of what research looks like in an institution committed to democratic experimentalism. As we made clear in the previous chapter, limiting ourselves to the gold standard of double-blind experiments with random assignment would mean doing away with entire swathes of careful learning, including non-experimental statistical models, more qualitative research, or even implicit knowledge generated by teachers, students, and other stakeholders as they carry out of their daily routines.

From there, we turn to the tricky question of how to create an informative knowledge base from findings of variable depth and precision. Using Bayesian inference as an inspiration, we demonstrate how different kinds of research can be used to change the way we look at the world. All evidence is worth considering, but some evidence is more convincing and more disruptive than others.

We close with a more practical concern: How can inquiry be regulated to maximize the returns on investment, while protecting everyone involved from unnecessary risk and undue departures from best practices?

What Counts as Research?

Scientists increasingly acknowledge that experimentation with random assignment is the ideal methodology for the social sciences, mainly because it minimizes selection bias and builds causal order into the research design. Indeed, Dorf and Sabel come dangerously close to arguing that it is the only form of inquiry allowed under their form of democratic experimentalism, and others have argued explicitly that we should evaluate policy only with rigorous experimental research designs.[1] We feel this approach is overly restrictive. Consider how difficult it is to design such experiments in the world of public policy. As cases in point, we present two of the most hotly debated large-scale social experiments in recent times.

In the 1990s the Moving to Opportunity for Fair Housing experiment set out to evaluate the effect of neighbourhoods on the life outcomes of residents. After finding volunteers who lived in high-poverty neighbourhoods in five major US cities,[2] the study randomly assigned participants to one of three groups. Everyone except the control group received vouchers towards a new residence. One treatment group could use the voucher anywhere, including in the neighbourhood where they already lived. The other treatment group had to use their voucher in a low-poverty neighbourhood. With this design, scientists could see whether moving from a high-poverty neighbourhood to a low-poverty neighbourhood made any difference in people's lives.[3] In the end, it seemed that moving to a different neighbourhood did very little,[4] a result that was surprising to those familiar with the literature on neighbourhood effects, and a confused debate emerged in the aftermath of the publication of the early findings.[5] The problem, as Robert Sampson pointed out, is that to evaluate neighbourhood effects you really need to randomize which neighbourhoods are good and which are bad – by, say, inducing some neighbourhoods, through increased investment, to improve. But the Moving to Opportunity experiment only randomized which people could move to a better neighbourhood.[6] Although the findings were clear, they did not answer the questions that many researchers thought were most relevant.

Another recent example of the gold-standard experimental study is the Oregon Medicaid health experiment. In 2008 Oregon found money in its budget to expand Medicaid in the state to cover an additional ten thousand people. When ninety thousand qualified residents applied for the program, Oregon decided to turn an awkward situation into an experiment. It held a lottery to determine which people would be given coverage and which would be left out – in essence, randomizing the selection of a treatment group and a control group. Four years later the initial results were released.[7] The specific findings are not especially important, except from a political standpoint. Some measures showed that Medicaid helped people, others showed it to be a waste of money. Some of these were statistically significant, while others were only substantively significant. This latter point caused a lot of consternation because of the sample size. Ten thousand is a healthy number for the study, and researchers were able to follow up with just under six thousand "winners." But most people never have to use their insurance for more than routine visits. To see whether Medicaid leads to better health outcomes, we need to be able to see people who actually use the program, and it turns out that the sample of people who were at risk of needing to use their Medicaid in the first year of the program was very small – small enough that it was hard to reach a level of statistical significance. So how should we interpret the results of the Oregon Medicaid health experiment? It is hard to say. Even if the data show no statistically significant effect, it might be worth taking that interpretation with a small-sample-sized grain of salt. We should also avoid going too far in the other direction and infer relationships where the data are inconclusive. But it is worth bearing in mind that the available data might not reveal every relevant relationship.

Even when experiments provide analytical clarity, there might be factors that muddy the results. Asking the wrong questions or not having a large enough sample size will cast a shadow on any research, experimental or otherwise. In the end, even though there are meaningful differences, there is no rigid dividing line between an experiment and other kinds of research. We argue that it is inappropriate to treat experimental (or even quasi-experimental) research as the *only* way to go forward for an institution, as Campbell and Dorf and Sabel do.[8]

Such an attitude would lead us to overlook the bulk of scientific research today, research that could otherwise be leveraged to improving our social policies. All kinds of inquiry can add to our understanding of the world, even the personal experiences of people on the ground. We need to ask: What does a study add to our current knowledge, and how much does it add? Controlled experiments are the best method available for evaluating causality, but there is worthwhile information that is not causal. Other quantitative methods might reveal the correlations between variables in either a static frame or across a time-series, giving us at least a look at what causal forces *might* be involved; and ethnographies and conversation analysis provide us with rich details about what is happening at the microscopic level of analysis. We could go on, but the point is that this is all information we can use, whether to guide further inquiry or to refine our current understandings. The advantages of a rigorous experimental design are real, but so are those of other kinds of research, even if they often bring less to the table.

To make a little more sense of this, think back to the way various pragmatists have approached the matter of inquiry, and how they have treated it as a matter of everyday life. Scientists might deploy a more rigorous and sophisticated form of inquiry, but it exists on a continuum with the activities in which teachers and students – and, for that matter, people in their everyday lives – engage. People learn from their circumstances – some better than others – and adjust their behaviour accordingly to meet their goals. Jane Addams tried to make things a little easier by using an alternative meaning of the word "experiment." In her view, every social intervention is an experiment in that each represents our best attempt to address some practical challenge that is subject to a continuously evolving universe.[9] As writers, we thought long and hard about using "experiment" in this way, since it is convenient shorthand that gets at much of the meaning we wish to convey. But ultimately we decided that the term carried too much baggage, and we did not want readers confusing one meaning of the word with another. We thus rely on terms such as inquiry and research, even when we argue that all our policy proposals need to be seen as tentative and, in its broadest sense, experimental.

The key here is that, in a complex world, we can use all the help we can get.[10] It makes little sense to discard the bulk of our knowledge, flawed though it might be; instead we advocate for an approach rooted in Bayesian induction. If you assume that we have some level of confidence in a statement such as "students learn chemistry most effectively through cooking," then new research will strengthen this confidence, weaken it, or leave it unaffected, all in varying degrees. An experiment with random assignment that finds in favour of the belief might substantially improve our confidence, while comparative-historical research on the role of cooking in childhood socialization might bolster it only slightly. But both cases have something to contribute. One tenet of an inquiring institution ought to be that there is no such thing as throwaway data.

Inductive Scaling

We use this same inductive approach to determine how best to expand or contract ongoing research. An institution hoping to generate knowledge through inquiry needs to establish the parameters for scaling existing projects. It needs to be able to say why a given research project should include so many towns, schools, or classrooms, and why it should grow or shrink as time passes and data are collected, so that resources and risk are distributed along clear lines. Dedicating too many classrooms and too many resources to exploring an idea can help bad ideas persist and marginalize good ideas. It can also expose more people to an inferior education or, at the very least, limit their access to best practices.

For the past few decades, outcomes-based education (OBE) has intrigued policy makers for the same reason. Like inductive scaling, the logic of OBE involves initiating creative efforts at the local level and working backwards to establish the curriculum, materials, teaching methods, and remedial activities that would increase the number of students who achieve success on desired learning outcomes. This requires gathering inputs of all kinds in order to evaluate whether or not an intervention leads to positive outcomes. At the same time, OBE traditionally has valued teacher accountability and the retention of students, making it attractive to parents as well.[11] OBE argues that we should increase the time and resources dedicated to helping students (especially struggling students) achieve pre-established learning outcomes.

Using Bayesian induction to inform resource allocation works in a similar way. Justified confidence is based on a probabilistic relationship between confidence and error, making for a game of maximization and minimization. High confidence in one technique entails a low probability of failure and wasted resources, while low confidence in another entails a high probability of both. Our confidence levels can be wrong in the end (resulting in increased harm or decreased benefits), but in general, because confidence is built upon pre-existing knowledge, providing empirical backing for baseline expectations, it should accurately predict success with reasonable consistency.

In technical terms, Bayesian confirmation theory is an attempt to use probability theory to evaluate rationally the impact of new evidence on existing beliefs.[12] It argues that we should think in terms of degrees of belief, rather than treating belief as a categorical value. Someone might believe that $3 + 5 = 8$ and that Sasquatch exists, but this does not mean that they treat both beliefs equally. They might be only 78 per cent sure that Sasquatch is stomping through the forests of British Columbia, but 99 per cent sure that $3 + 5 = 8$. New evidence, of course, could change this level of confidence. Our cryptozoologist might encounter an article that shows how the footprints he believes to belong to Sasquatch are really grizzly tracks. Because the article does not comprehensively refute the cryptozoologist, we might expect him to retain a level of confidence in the reality of Sasquatch, but he might now be only 64 per cent sure that the creature exists. New evidence has forced him to reconsider things, but it has not collapsed his view of the world. He is, after all, a respectable cryptozoologist.

In the same vein, philosopher Alvin Goldman suggests that truth comes in degrees, and although we draw more heavily on Bayes, we would be remiss if we failed to mention our debt to Goldman as well. Beliefs can be more or less truth-like, or "veritistic," in his words.[13] From this observation, he goes on to explore how we can revise the process of public discourse, scientific inquiry, and the institutional trappings of law to raise the truth-quality of their products. Social epistemology has emerged as a field of inquiry to respond further to the questions Goldman raises.[14] The applicability of Goldman's views to our vision of a scientifically sound educational system is immediately obvious. Since theories of learning have many moving parts, it is extremely difficult to pick out what is accurate from what is a little bit off. With that in mind, by adopting a more lenient approach to truth and falsity, we can encourage people to adopt empirically supported methods without overreaching.

The theory is straightforward, but calculating the change in confidence (or its veritistic value) that we should experience when new evidence becomes available requires that we know, or at least have a sense of, the level of confidence we held in the prior state of belief and the degree to which the new evidence supports (or fails to support) that belief. Because there is no consensus on how to calculate these two quantities, we can use the Bayesian confirmation theory only to guide our effort to delineate procedures for scaling experiments.

Luckily there are still some concrete things we can say about the method. First, to establish a level of confidence, we need to rely heavily on data already accumulated in previous experiments, inside the institution and out. In so doing, we eliminate some of the subjective bias associated with estimates of future experimental results, and we are able to assign value to a project based on existing knowledge. Second, although the degree of confidence in an experiment can increase incrementally as it employs successively larger and more refined samples, the process does not necessarily begin at 1 per cent and finish at 99 per cent. (Since we are treating confidence as non-absolute, neither 0 per cent nor 100 per cent is attainable.) In fact, these two poles rarely come into play in inquiry, as 1 per cent represents an extreme belief in failure and 99 per cent an extreme belief in success. That said, most projects would borrow something from the scientific literature, either transposing expectations from a previous experiment to public space or adapting applicable findings in novel ways, thereby introducing a layer of uncertainty that influences the degree of confidence. As new data become available over time, the degree of confidence will increase, decrease, or remain steady.

Confidence itself, however, is insufficient to establish the scale for research; it needs to be balanced by considerations of risk. Relying on confidence alone to justify scaling decisions might saddle the institution with unforeseen costs – financial costs to the institution or less tangible costs to the people it serves. The institution can protect itself against the fallout from failure, however, by developing contingency plans after evaluating the various avenues along which damage might accrue. Note that when analysts refer to risk, they typically mean the probability that an undesirable event will occur, along with some measure of its severity.[15] We have already sectioned off part of the probability question by determining the degree of confidence accorded an experiment. Here, we are mainly concerned about the variation in the severity of consequences from experiment to experiment.

There is no simple inverse relation between confidence and risk. If there were, an institution could scale experiments with only its expectations of success in mind. Instead, some experiments carry more risk than others because of differences in expense and potential danger to participants. Introducing digital simulations to five classrooms to help teach biology, for instance, carries much more financial risk than modifying the curriculum of the same five classrooms to speak more to the features of local ecosystems. Pharmaceutical interventions carry health risks that most kinesthetic learning initiatives do not. Similarly, the risk of diminished educational quality is differentially distributed across experiments. Although this risk can be managed to some extent by the measure of confidence, loss of educational quality is difficult to predict because of the complexity of social environments. Unquantifiable risks such as these must also factor into the analysis, despite our tenacious discomfort with uncertainty.

Considerations of risk inflect the basic relationship between confidence and scale. If, for the sake of simplicity, we assume that scale is positively (and linearly) related to confidence, then variations in risk serve to further refine the level of scale assigned to each project. This works both ways: high-risk research can be reduced in scale compared to expectations based on the degree of confidence, and low-risk research can be increased in scale.

Because study design can fit the existing data in better and worse ways, risk needs to be both examined before a project is launched and re-examined over the course of its implementation. People responsible for evaluating risk might be willing to call tentatively for the inclusion of sixteen classrooms in the sample, based on a research proposal. But they might lower that number to seven if methodological problems are encountered over the following months – for example, if researchers have been unable to locate classrooms with appropriate demographics to test their hypothesis, and propose settling for less-than-ideal research contexts. Scale should be modified in these cases, because the alternative is to increase risk in the face of decreased methodological quality.

This basic model also has implications for knowledge management.[16] Statistical relationships might suggest that confidence levels be revised as new data validate or invalidate them. Over time these new data will allow researchers to identify how changing social and cultural patterns are modifying the operation of various techniques. Practitioners will be able to use the data to determine their best options for intervening in specific situations.

Regulating Inquiry

Exposing students to inferior educational practices through well-intentioned research can subtly influence life outcomes.[17] In any educational context, safeguards need to be in place to protect students from eccentric personalities and bad ideas; in a truly experimental context, this protection should include whatever steps are necessary to mitigate any potential risk.

In any scientific investigation, regulation begins with methods for refining the theory and methodology of prospective projects. On its own, peer review is insufficient. Although it evolved within the academic community to maximize the quality of the finished product, and was adapted for ethical concerns in the form of the institutional review board, it has no inherent ability, for example, to distribute samples of students among research projects according to their merit. The institution needs to regulate matters such as distribution in order to minimize risk because, in addition to capitalizing on new data, the school system serves as the research site. Researchers should have access to larger sample sizes only when they can demonstrate that existing knowledge validates the risk and only when experts are confident that the approach will be successful. Processes should be in place both to carry out this more intensive form of peer review and to allocate resources accordingly.

The choice of research projects and areas of study should be subject to regulation, as well. Inquiry needs to be constructed in collaboration with regional actors and, in many cases, in response to local concerns. But this diffusion of power – and possibly, but not necessarily, expertise – means that students could be exposed inadvertently to inferior practices because of local peculiarities. Imagine a school district that is possessed of the idea that student performance has everything to do with effort and nothing to do with family life, teacher quality, school resources, and so on. Left unchecked, this district might leverage its decision-making power to sponsor only research that addresses motivational aspects, and refuse to enforce emerging best-practice standards related to teaching. As a result, students from this district would graduate with a significant disadvantage in the labour market, in the workplace, and even in family life.

In conjunction with review and allocation processes, safeguards should be in place to prevent local authorities from using their power to advance ideas that have already been discounted by credible research. These safeguards would establish a balance of power to ensure that experiments conducted without scientific merit are blocked by the wider institution. They would also ensure that applications for retrials of clearly failed experiments are denied; once an experiment yields clearly negative data, those data should be used to justify denial. This is not to say that we should foreclose the possibility of novel experiments based on failed ideas if the data can help identify conditions for new experiments with potentially more promising outcomes. For instance, if the original experiment failed in a rural environment, there might be reasons to expect classrooms in suburban environments to respond differently.

To capitalize on numerous research projects occurring simultaneously in a school system committed to gathering evidence, local actors need to share the results of their projects so that decision makers elsewhere do not implement disproven initiatives or waste resources by testing well-established techniques. Making information on previous inquiry available to all localities would ensure that regions fully engaged in the research process are able to respond most appropriately to their situation. Any structure explicitly designed for sharing would need to manage an immense wealth of knowledge and assist local actors in parsing for relevant data. The school district above, for example, might be well intentioned in its single-minded effort to increase student motivation and be perfectly willing to scan available knowledge to adjust its understanding of the issues. Inverting the sharing process, it is also important to require local actors to seek out successful ideas from past research before setting new policy or initiating new inquiries. Minimally, this sharing process should be an informal requirement. Together, these considerations should encourage the creation of regionally specific but scientifically interesting research, while protecting students from both short-term and long-term harm.

We have already explicitly addressed the need to set standards for the incremental scaling of research, towards either widespread adoption or elimination, and the need for replication before widespread adoption because of the potential risk to students. This process can also be used to revise expectations about the applicability of a new idea. But before any of these decisions can be made, even with the data in hand, we need to define success in a way that all parties can accept. Research projects cannot be designed properly, let alone evaluated at their conclusion, unless some standard of success – in the form of measurables such as test scores and behavioural patterns – has been determined. Establishing clear metrics and indicators also helps mitigate the potential for disagreement. If disputes arise about future scaling decisions or project design, specific data would be available to settle them. Ambiguous data might suggest the project merits another run with minimal resources.

Nuances arising from data interpretation might call for further refining of methodology. Successful projects might require larger sample sizes in order for researchers to acquire higher levels of statistical confidence and to determine the scope of their applicability. For example, an idea might be effective with adolescent boys, but unhelpful with adolescent girls; decision makers would then need to decide how to revise the experiment to account for these differences. Similarly, successful research might be repurposed for new applications. Researchers might believe that an approach to teaching information science in university could change the way we teach chemistry in high school, and argue for the creation of new experiments to examine this possibility. Other inquiries will fail, and although in some cases this might mean eliminating the project entirely, more often than not it would qualify the expectations surrounding it, limiting future iterations along gender lines, socio-economic status, or other factors. Some grain of promise usually would remain.

The Ethics of Participation

Before we leave the topic of research inside the educational institution, we have one more matter to address: How can we justify the participation of thousands of students, teachers, administrators, parents, and communities in creative research that is thrust upon them by a universally mandated public institution? They are not volunteers. Exposing people to potential harm raises serious ethical questions.

It is tempting to begin by suggesting that contributing to the constant reform of an institution can be an inherently valuable experience for the people involved. They might come away feeling satisfied that they are helping to improve education (and society). But this is a superficial response that glosses over the variety of human experience. Some people will find participating in an experimental institution onerous; others will emerge confused and shaken. Although there might be principled benefits to engaging in the experimental process, planners cannot oversimplify the risk in order to deflect public concerns.

Without running roughshod over these concerns, some aspects of the institution should be made clear. What we describe in this book is an adjoining structure – the Epistemic Division – to the existing school system. The experiments it carries out would be used to generate knowledge that increases the overall efficiency and effectiveness of the broader education system. Research classrooms would not be the norm, but they would have an impact on the way generic classrooms operate. Research classrooms probably would need to make up a small portion of the total number of classrooms at any time. For the sake of argument, imagine supplementing 9,500 generic classrooms with 500 classrooms engaged in various research projects. The ethical issue of participation, then, would apply to perhaps 5 per cent of the classrooms in a region, along with whatever proportion of students, teachers, parents, and others who would be affected by an experiment. Most students would take part in only a handful of research classrooms over the duration of their time in school. As one branch of a larger institution, research classrooms would be a small, though still significant, part of the adaptive education system we envision.

The danger of harm to participants is real, but smaller than one might think, especially since many inquiries would result in only small gains or losses in educational quality. Meanwhile, students would benefit in the remainder – and the bulk – of their courses from knowledge gleaned through research. Even if the benefits of new knowledge for each individual classroom were minute, which is not entirely plausible (just as it is not entirely plausible to treat every risk as incremental), over time the aggregate would become noticeable.

Keep in mind, too, that some of the research classrooms would be an improvement over generic classrooms. Despite the risk associated with a research project, participating students would benefit from the research before the general student population, thereby obtaining a small advantage over their peers, although, over time, as more students participated in successful and creative research, this effect would cancel out. It is simply incorrect to treat novelty as harmful in itself. The average student would experience net gains – not unlike the case of universal education itself: although many people have noted that school systems carry dangers that home-schooling or autodidacticism do not, most of the population benefits from a streamlined educational system.

In the context of potential harm, it is worth considering what statisticians call type I and type II errors. Type I errors occur when we accept as true something that is in fact false. Type II errors, in contrast, occur when we reject something as false that is in fact true.[18] Generally, when the probability of one type of error decreases, the probability of the other increases. Because the severity of each type of error varies depending on the situation, each profession has its own way of balancing the costs and benefits of both. Failing to notice mechanical defects (a type II error) will have far more dangerous consequences than believing there is a defect when there is none (a type I error). Scientists prefer to maintain their body of knowledge by guarding against mistakenly including false information (a type I error) at the expense of overlooking some information that proves to be true (a type II error). For educators, as for scientists, the primary danger to research participants would stem from the failure to reject incorrect practices (a type I error), while the failure to recognize effective practices (a type II error) would merely obscure their main benefits. Experimenting institutions would be able to balance these errors in new ways. By limiting the number of courses involved in research (in addition to scaling according to confidence and risk), the impact of type I errors would be kept small, allowing the institution to lean towards minimizing type II errors as well and maximizing the potential benefits for everyone involved.

Despite the net benefits that would accrue to participants in an adaptive education institution, some people, after familiarizing themselves with its details or being briefed by researchers, might feel that a certain project is undesirable, and that they would rather enrol themselves or their children in a generic course. Accordingly, the right to refuse to participate should be protected. Opting-out procedures could take various forms, depending largely on the prevailing political climate surrounding the institution. It is unlikely that an institution would guarantee the limitless right to opt out because it would need participants to continue doing research (and because free riders are not popular). On the other hand, to refuse to allow opting out under any circumstances would be ethically indefensible. Most situations likely would require participation in a minimum number of inquiries, and limit the number of times an individual could opt out.

Since many students might opt out of an experimental course, it seems likely that volunteers would step forward. This option, however, should be applied discriminately. Research sites would be chosen because their specific composition would help test the guiding hypothesis, and just as opting out might change this composition, so those who wish to opt in might not fit the project's profile. Moreover, the type of person who would volunteer to participate in creative pedagogies or programs might bias the results. Accordingly, researchers would have to vet potential participants thoroughly to avoid this problem. One solution might be to place volunteers in a pool of potential replacements, rather than to guarantee their participation.

In our discussion of scaling and ethics, we have focused mainly on the potential to maximize improvement in the technical aspects of education and minimize the risks involved with limited data. But the advantages of encouraging more adaptation in education are not limited to the science of teaching. Social programs in schools are equally valid testing grounds for new ideas, although they possess a wrinkle that technical teaching practices do not: policies might infringe on our right to choose or contain implicit moral and political content that some find offensive. It thus would not be enough to account for risk in these cases; it would be equally important to manage the diverse opinions represented in the local population.[19]

Imagine that schools, nationally, were suffering from dangerous levels of bullying and that both educators and parents recognized the severity of the issue, and pledged to develop possible solutions in conjunction with local communities. Suppose the most popular suggestion was to have all students participate in an alternative drama program that asks them to take on the role of the victim in a series of scenes. Afterwards, their performance is evaluated with the school counsellor for hidden assumptions and unhealthy expectations. Some stakeholders, however, might withhold their support over concerns that, by not singling out bullies, the school system was glossing over their behaviour and helping them avoid punishment. By gradually increasing the scale of the project over time, however, we could avoid bulldozing those concerns while still collecting meaningful data that could be used to further the debate. Researchers might limit the project to five or ten schools in the first experimental run, and find that the data strongly support wider implementation. After data are collected over multiple iterations of the study, with various sample sizes, it might become clear that bullies respond extremely well to this type of intervention, and emerge with a better appreciation of the damage they do by bullying. Although some might reoffend, many might change their behaviour. Stakeholders, both those who initially supported the project and those who did not, would then be forced to confront new data in public forums where the debate could be resolved. If the data showed marked benefits with limited downsides, especially if they addressed the concerns of stakeholders, wider implementation of the project could be approved. The converse would also apply: if the data validated prominent concerns and did not mitigate them with dramatic benefits, the experimental social project could be discontinued.

This example presents a fairly idealized version of public debate. Data will never solve all of our issues, for the simple reason that many people – perhaps all of us – are too committed to certain beliefs to accept invalidating evidence. We cannot assume that all stakeholders are committed to following empirical data, whichever way they lead. Instead, the process needs to be governed by something like a contract that would stipulate that, to participate in generating and critiquing experiments, stakeholders must agree to respect the findings presented in the data. Interpretations of results can differ, of course, and all scientific judgments are biased in some sense. But an experimenting institution cannot allow participants to disregard the data it produces. To oversimplify, if research shows that X is related to Y, stakeholders cannot deny the relationship; if they want to reject the findings, they must point to a failure of methodology, analysis, or interpretation.

The Institution in Transition

Closing the existing gap between research and practice in the context of an adaptive education model would require a period of transition and willingness to relearn roles and relationships both within and outside the institution. To that end, we introduce here the concept of "buttressing," which refers to the need for related institutions to undergo reform in ways that are mutually supporting and that build on one another's emerging strengths. In an open social context, related institutions exist in a state of balance, in which their practices and expectations align with one another and with public expectations. Introducing reform in one institution or one part of an institution shifts that balance. The natural response to imbalance is to seek equilibrium, and an easy solution is to slip back into the comfort of habitual behaviour, leading to stagnation. We see buttressing as a way to direct that search away from stagnation and towards continual reform.

Buttressing would play a somewhat ambiguous role in our reform process. Since it would encourage institutional interdependence and help to combat the pressures that lead to stagnation, we might expect it to hasten the transition. But since its primary advantages include achieving and maintaining balance with surrounding institutions, complementing the habits and understandings of the population, and thereby moving both the public and relevant professionals towards a new reality, it would have the simultaneous effect of encouraging incremental adjustments at the expense of transformational reform.

Retraining teachers and shifting professional expectations create a similar ambiguity. An institution cannot change its relationship with its charges overnight, nor can it assign new tasks and responsibilities to staff without altering the nature of their jobs. New professional standards require new certification and professional development programs, at least for incoming cohorts. But this is not enough. To bridge the gap and to avoid a culture clash between new and more experienced teachers, existing teachers must be given enough resources to fill their roles adequately in the meantime. This process, like buttressing, encourages incremental change. Buttressing and (re)training programs, however, are only two of many possibilities for managing transition. Another transitional approach is to build successive reforms on one another, moving towards closer approximations slowly so that people and surrounding institutions can familiarize themselves with the changes over time.

Our emphasis on transition is not meant to imply that adaptive education would be confined to an intermediate stage; on the contrary, we see it as an ideal. By focusing on transition, however, we hope to make it easier to envision moving towards adaptive education in various contexts. For example, if a local region were implementing an experimental model supportive of government interventions, adaptive education initiatives might use buttressing to rely on public institutions that deal with demography, statistics, scientific grants, and so on. On the other hand, should an area be committed to small government, the new initiative might instead use private research firms as buttresses to supply the same services, perhaps charging tuition to cover the costs. In both cases, systems would rely on established, parallel structures to move them towards an experimental model.

Changes in the teaching profession, too, might take different transitional paths, depending on the existing environment. In a country like Finland, for example, where certification requirements are set fairly high, professional standards might need only to incorporate an appreciation for experimentation, but regional cultures where teaching is overwhelmingly informed by tradition and instinct would need considerable adjustments for adaptive education to flourish. Choosing to examine the intermediate stages involved in reform would allow the model to be modified according to situational needs.

5 Learning to Teach

In the past few chapters we have considered the nature of inquiry, its basis in normal human behaviour, how it works in groups, and how we can use these insights to design institutions that are responsive to changing environments. Since our goal is to improve the quality and relevance of education by tying teachers and other local stakeholders more tightly to the research process, we turn now to examine the role of teachers and teaching in our adaptive education model.

We begin by reinforcing a point we made earlier, and will return to in Chapter 6: we need to open avenues that allow and encourage teachers to participate in the inquiry process. Suffice it to say here that pragmatism – at least in the particular incarnation we have been tracing from Dewey and Follett through to Unger, Dorf, and Sabel – legitimizes the contributions of local actors. Their experiences provide a valuable resource for developing creative interventions for problems that arise in and around the educational institution.

However, teachers need not only to participate in the inquiry process, but also to learn from it and to implement new ideas in their regular practice, and for this to occur we need to introduce methods that prepare them for inquiry-based teaching. Although pre-service teacher training introduces key findings about learning and pedagogy, when teachers arrive in the classroom they often turn to instinct to guide their efforts. If we incorporate teachers into the framework of institutionalized inquiry without simultaneously changing the way people learn to teach, it is possible that nothing will change despite our best intentions. That is the challenge we unpack in this chapter.

Typically, students are admitted into a teacher education program, where they receive an additional degree and teacher certification, after they have completed their undergraduate work. Sometimes teacher training occurs in conjunction with an undergraduate degree in what is referred to as a co-curricular or concurrent degree. Once new teachers begin their teaching careers, they benefit from informal interactions, training, and support from more seasoned colleagues, but there is rarely time for new teachers to evaluate their own practice – to hold it up to the light of their academic training. And so, gradually, they turn increasingly to their own instincts and to advice from peers. Of course, we recognize that, in addition to pre-service teacher training and the wisdom of colleagues, teachers can – and often do – take advantage of professional development opportunities throughout their careers, including additional formal education in graduate school and/or in-service workshops that address specific topics.

Although we believe newly designed methods for teachers, administrators, and education specialists should include existing practices such as pre-service teacher training programs, professional development seminars, and administrative evaluations, we argue that they should also include the production (and updating) of diagnostic and best practices documentation, and professional expectations around keeping up with current findings through official documentation and professional journals.

It is equally important to consider the informal training that takes place both on the job and away from the job. As we saw earlier, people in all walks of life learn from one another and solve problems together when they engage in shared practices with shared goals. Teachers are no different; informal communities of practice, many of which already exist, allow teachers to share experiences, successes, and failures. Without a solid grounding in inquiry, however, they might also reinforce bad habits as well as good ones.

Before we delve too deeply into this topic, we should pause and consider what teachers are and what they do. We have come a long way from the authoritarian figure standing in front of neat rows of students. But many people (and probably some readers!) still hold this image. It is worth our time to make it clear what we mean when we talk about the teaching profession.

What Is a Teacher, Anyway?

The concepts of teaching as speaking and learning as listening have shifted. Today most academics and professionals in education view

teaching as the process of facilitating learning, a view shared by pragmatists and based on observations of the learning that is part of everyday life.[1] It has been incorporated into so many variants of teaching that
we easily forget how influential it has been, but pedagogical theorists
recognize the indelible mark of experiential learning on both thought
and practice in education. In this regard, there is no more important
reference point – in North America, at least – than John Dewey or,
depending on one's social scientific proclivities, Kurt Lewin, Jean
Piaget, or Lev Vygotsky.[2]

According to the experiential theories these thinkers espoused,
learning occurs as action unfolds. In one sense this relationship is
trivial, since – as one of Dewey's immediate predecessors in pragmatism, foundational psychologist William James, notes – we are always
acting.[3] To say that learning occurs as action unfolds is akin to saying that change happens in the course of time. These are truisms. But
there is another, more meaningful interpretation of this statement.
We often think of education as separate from the "real world," as if
meaningful action begins only once we move out of the classroom.
The stuff we learn is seen as informing our actions, rather than both
informing and emerging from our actions. This depiction is the hand-
me-down of rational choice thinking, which argues that humans
act based on what they have learned and thought through. Planned
learning, in this mindset, is a special sort of activity that is (somewhat)
separate from everyday learning. Pragmatism counters this reasoning
by arguing that learning is the prototypical human activity: students
can learn just as well about biology from expeditions to local parks as
they can from textbooks and lectures. Learning is a matter of enlarg-
ing the range of life experiences.

Once we understand learning as the process of incorporating creative solutions into our habitual repertoires, it follows that learning
begins with creativity. This is important, because actions range in creative content from the minute adjustment of habits from one situation
to the next to upheavals of entire habitual complexes, as we saw in
the example of the missing bedroom door. Traditional educational
approaches that rely on lecture and rote memorization force only
minimal change. Dewey advocated the use of novel situations to spur
learning, giving students little recourse to existing habit and forcing
them to invent or transpose responses for the situation at hand. For
example, at his laboratory school, Dewey had students learn chemistry through cooking.[4] He thought that the processes of adding heat

or agitating ingredients to induce chemical reactions helped make the subject matter real to students. More generically, consider the value of field trips. Although it would be silly to attribute their origin to pragmatism – the field trip can be traced in some form all the way to antiquity – its continued popularity owes much to experiential learning. Field trips provide hands-on experiences that allow for the development of more abstract thinking.[5]

Like any other theory with broad applicability, experiential learning has a number of offshoots. Problem-based learning, which has become influential in most corners of educational practice,[6] was first developed in medicine to help students recognize the relevance of the curriculum to their daily lives and course of study, engaging them in the creation of knowledge by asking them to solve problems related to the subject matter. Problems typically have more than one solution, so students are forced to employ critical thinking, rather than obscure information, in developing their responses. These ventures can be traced back to Dewey.[7]

Other pedagogical approaches, also linked to pragmatism, focus on the world beyond the walls of the classroom. Service learning asks students to apply what they learn to projects that help the community. In this way, experiential learning is activated through novel situations, and students are taught civic values and to observe the benefits in the neighbourhood – for instance, by way of an urban bike trail.[8] Service learning has become extremely popular in environmental education, since it simultaneously accomplishes curricular goals and works towards sustainability.[9] One especially interesting example is the increasingly popular farmer field school. Farmers, both established and aspiring, in impoverished regions are brought together to learn about state-of-the-art techniques pertaining to everything from crop rotation and fertilization to pesticides. The courses typically emphasize hands-on experience, sometimes taking advantage of practice fields donated by local farmers. These schools have proved effective in promoting better farming techniques (improving yields and quality) and reducing rural poverty.[10]

Pragmatism and Dewey are most closely associated with Adult Education, whether in private organizations or in the school system. Developmentally, the pragmatist theory of action is about adults. This is not to say that Dewey and others had no conception of how children behave,[11] but the primary difference between children and adults lies in life experience. Since children cannot draw on life experience, they have trouble categorizing raw information – hence their natural love of exploration and inquiry. If the active search is removed from the classroom, children not only suffer from lack of motivation, they also learn far less. Adults, on the other hand, enter the classroom with vast stores of personal experience; they cannot (or, rather, will not) dissociate themselves from pre-existing interests and challenges. They want to see how their learning can help them in their daily lives, in raising their kids, paying their bills, advancing their careers, and getting along with their neighbours. To accomplish these goals, they do not need to run from one experimental sandbox to another. Since people develop their capacity for deliberative thought over time, adult learners are able to apply this cognitive, problem-solving skill to adjust habits related to their real lives.[12]

In effective learning environments, students are not passive receivers and teachers are not droning lecturers. The pragmatist theory of action implies that students should be allowed to experiment, rather than accept uncritically the answers presented to them by teachers and text-books. Of course, teachers and course content are still relevant to the learning process. Emulation is one common way of developing creative solutions; for young children, it is often the main avenue for learning. But new information needs to be reified in action, whether as an object of thought, part of the definition of the situation, or in communication. By encouraging experimentation, we increase the potential for transforming students' habits.

Let's look at a hypothetical teacher. Twenty-five years ago, he started his first job as a grade 8 teacher in a local middle school. He chose this profession because it allowed him to continue to practise his passion for music by teaching music appreciation, band, and ethnomusicology. How should he teach? One approach would be to ask his students to appreciate the music that he values and listens to regularly. Our teacher did just this, insisting that students listen to and study Wagner, Tchaikovsky, Mozart, and Bach. For all their technical wizardry, however, the classical composers failed to capture the imagination of most students

Then, our teacher went back to school to earn an MA in education. He learned all sorts of newfangled ideas, and became concerned with establishing processes that foster classroom interaction and, practically speaking, with maintaining an awareness of the community and developments in the adolescent and young adult music scene. When he returned to his classroom, he presented musical tastes, which are bundles of habits, as questions with no right or wrong answers – and this open-endedness created the opportunity for students to experiment and co-construct knowledge. The widely varying tastes that students brought to the classroom served as the organizing point for crafting learning opportunities. Together the class worked to produce a score for the latest songs in the Top 40, and learned to play "Bohemian Rhapsody." Our astute teacher took the opportunity to point out classical influences on the pieces. In the end music was operationalized as a hybrid combination of discipline, vocation, and hobby, an expansive definition that was arrived at collectively.

Teachers are designers of creative learning experiences. Sometimes traditional methods work. In many cases – in some branches of physics, for example – there are no good analogues in everyday life, and memorization and drills are the most helpful way forward. But in many other situations, students benefit from more active and creative learning environments, and teachers need to be ready to move away from lesson planning to something more like experience engineering.

None of this is especially controversial in theory. But there is a significant gap between theoretical perspectives on learning and teaching and classroom practices, in part because creating experiential learning experiences is just plain hard work, and going with our instincts is the path of least resistance. But with focused training, it is possible to take strides in the right direction.

Customizing Standards

In crafting effective learning experiences for their students, teachers benefit from cutting-edge knowledge. But it is never a straightforward procedure to apply findings gleaned elsewhere to our immediate surroundings, because local situations have peculiarities that defy generalization. For this reason best practices need to be expressed in abstract terms; no teacher should be expected to implement best practices exactly as they are expressed in theory. To ensure they fit specific conditions, standards should be customized to apply in real life.[13]

Individuals and communities benefit overall when teachers tune their efforts to the specific needs of each student. This implies a move towards individualizing the curriculum and adjusting the way we teach for every student. Some programs around the world aim for just this, but expanding individualization to apply to every student can be prohibitive, in terms of both expense and the demands it places on teachers.

We propose, instead, using empirically determined best practices to customize at some higher organizational level – the school, neighbourhood, and even city or region[14] – while encouraging instructors to make appropriate adjustments in their own classrooms. There are enough salient differences at these more aggregated levels to make customization possible. For instance, if the proportion of students from families with low socio-economic status were high in the aggregate, we could draw on data to find techniques to address that demographic. If we had trouble finding features to guide customization for a particular demographic, we could search for practices with high levels of generalized success.

Using existing empirical data to justify customization would increase the likelihood of success, but it would not eliminate the possibility for failure. Not only are there confounding factors, but each factor also includes variations of its own. Boys might respond well to using drama to teach math, but in saying this we do not mean *every* boy, but the *average* boy. Over thousands of classrooms, overall quality would increase, but because environmental factors are to some degree artificial categories, it is important to rely on teachers to make adjustments. They are far better acquainted with individual students than are people removed from the situation, and they are able to decide if the boys in their class are, in fact, *average* boys. This selective customization, based on teachers' experience and taking account of the nuances of the classroom, would help guard against the misapplication of research.

Attention to local nuances also would demand changes in the way classrooms are organized and run. Over time, research would shape the knowledge base available to teachers and administrators, providing them with empirical data to support their interventions. Such information is unavoidably complex, pointing to various interlacing factors that change the way people respond to specific methods and environmental features. Because of this complexity, research-based education needs to rely on the situational familiarity of specific local actors – namely, teachers. Finding appropriate solutions would rely on the ability of the practitioner to identify the factors at play. How will individual students respond to a particular method? Are they confident enough to lead their own educational experience, or do they need guidance? Will taking students out of their comfort zone lead them to a breakthrough, or will it cause them to become withdrawn? Only the familiarity that comes with repeated life experience can answer these questions.

Formal Training and Evaluation

It goes almost without saying that students do better when they have exceptional teachers. The authors of a significant study in New York City found that students taught by high-value-added teachers in the early grades had better life outcomes, higher levels of post-secondary attendance, and higher earnings.[15] Value-added analysis, which involves measuring a teacher's contribution in a given year by comparing the current test scores of his or her students to the scores of those same students in previous school years, to the scores of other students in the same grade, and to predicted scores, continues to bear this out.[16] Unfortunately, although value-added analysis confirms the importance of teaching, it contributes to a punitive undercurrent that has captured the much of the public narrative about education. The good news is that good teaching can be learned, and the widespread public interest it generates can lead to additional resources. There is no need to use punitive tools or to fire underperforming teachers; value-added analysis would be better used for training purposes.

The United States seems particularly keen on producing alternative programs to regular teacher education. Teach for America, for example, trains high-achieving undergraduates as prospective teachers in low-income communities, with the reasonable assumption that smarter students make for smarter teachers. But their training takes place over a mere five weeks. My Brother's Keeper is an initiative to help African-American and Hispanic boys in inner-city schools who are said to face inexperienced teachers as one of their many educational issues. Lacking either certainty about the underlying assumption of incompetent teachers or congruence among the solutions, it is little wonder that the United States has established a national dialogue – termed RESPECT (Recognizing Educational Success, Professional Excellence, and Collaborative Teaching) – about transforming education for the twenty-first century, which features research-based discussions of teacher education and the use of well-timed evaluations.

So how do we make better teachers? Instead of overturning what needs to be merely tweaked, we argue that it is possible to support teachers' education and professional development by coupling existing resources more tightly. We could start by treating teaching ability as a skill that develops with experience and effort (and regresses without them), rather than as a fixed personal trait. So-called master teaching programs move us in this direction by combining teacher training and researcher inquiry. They demand that graduates have a solid handle on their teaching pedagogical philosophies and use practica to hone their craft. Understandably this training can take some time to complete.

Research appears to support the importance of teacher education, which is by far the strongest correlate of student achievement.[17] The first few years of teaching experience also have a profound impact on novice teachers' professional development.[18] More research is needed to assess what teachers learn in their pedagogical preparation programs and the relationship of that knowledge to subsequent teacher behaviour and student learning,[19] but an early consensus is already forming.

Learning to teach can be seen as a process of developing a personal methodology for addressing daily life as a teacher. Basic to this process is an acquaintance with current research findings. Math teachers, for instance, might have an intuition that students can be helped to learn trigonometry if it tied to their physical experiences, but sending them out to measure a flagpole does not work very well. A new way to approach teaching trigonometry might be research that suggests that using our bodies to mimic the shape of triangles and the movement of wave functions encourages deeper learning.[20]

Constructing a database dedicated to compiling research findings would be an important first step in moving the teaching profession to evidence-based practice. To make access to that database easier for teachers, we suggest incorporating it into a handbook of teaching practices, explaining research on creative practices and detailing the situations for which they might be appropriate. Timely seminars and workshops on key topics could help address issues that arise in local environments. For more intractable problems, teachers could be encouraged to consult with experts on the substantive issue and possibilities for deeper investigation, or even take part in an ongoing inquiry. All of these tools would be the outcomes of an experimenting institution that incorporates state-of-the-art practices at a steady rate with the goal of maximizing educational quality over time.

In order for personal methodologies to incorporate field experiences and practica, new and pre-service teachers need to experience them first-hand and understand what they look like. An international analysis of trends in the teaching profession in twenty-five countries found that, in a typical classroom, the main distraction from time "in the front of the classroom" is the presence of questions and problems that cannot be accurately predetermined.[21] This finding reminds us that teaching is inherently problem based – an important lesson that should predispose us towards research as a way to find solutions. The study also noted that field experience as a part of teacher training is both more frequent and more varied than in the past. These opportunities should be continued, since they augment pre-service teachers' ability to empathize with broader social issues. Careful unpacking of this experience would provide excellent opportunities for learning about the connections between social issues and schools. Community-service learning pedagogies are designed for learning in such contexts, and the student is usually the focus of learning. In terms of retraining experienced teachers, however, something akin to community service learning could disrupt expectations enough to promote new ways of approaching the profession.

It is also important to develop guidelines for teachers to follow in addressing individual students' needs. How do you invite students to share their issues? How do you detect the true nature of the problem? How do you communicate the need for lag time between hearing and answering a question if you do not know the answer? If both you and the student need to conduct research, how do you explain the effort required? If the question is more broadly applicable to the entire class, how do you either credit the student or shield her from possible criticism? Do you allocate time each day for personal investigations of emerging issues? Is your personal methodology communicated to students so that they know what to expect?

In sum, we propose the development of a personal methodology to be institutionalized in the teacher education program, along with an accompanying set of professional tools whose content links to specific techniques and best practices. As a starting point, teachers should be exposed to techniques for accessing relevant research and best practices. This is surprisingly difficult given the myriad types of marginal literature that flood the research space. Our solution is a database dedicated to this issue, but even here users would need to understand how to extrapolate and apply the findings and recommendations to particular situations. Learning how to do this in a problem-based setting is one possibility. The personal methodology should also encompass a set of principles relating to interactions with students and others in the environment; for example, a logical expansion could include applying the classroom approach to parents' questions.

In the process of developing their methodology, budding teachers should tailor their principles to their discipline, in anticipation of the types of questions they are likely to encounter. To support the development of personal methodologies in pre-service teachers, it would be crucial for teacher education programs to foster feedback mechanisms, perhaps in the form of a peer review process that helps teachers learn from one another. The use of diagnostic tools would be another friendly evaluation strategy, easing the transition into a world of steady feedback.

A teacher education program that adopted an experimental approach and prepared its graduates by creating the courses and other experiences necessary to support that approach would be a key vehicle for formalizing the model we promote. Ideally, coursework would be problem based and require student-teacher involvement in a research study. Practica would combine classroom and other experiences. Inquiry and experimentation would be persistent themes across the program, and students would take a course or courses on basic educational research. In addition, to cap off their pre-service training, students would be required to develop their personal methodology as it relates to the database and best-practices handbook. The program would also feature a required seminar series, bringing the real world of education into students' lives on a weekly basis. Administrators, politicians, union representatives, and educational organizations would discuss their ties to and thoughts on education in gatherings that would replicate the kinds of outreach necessary to generate ideas on educational research.

Collaborative Learning and the Community of Practice

When we think about implementing new training programs for teachers, most of us gravitate towards formal changes such as the ones we have just discussed. But just as important, if not more so, is the informal learning that takes place in and around the workplace. People learn from their experiences and from one another in conversation or from observation. This is one reason that research on teacher education programs has a more limited impact on practice than designers would like. The peer review method we mention above would be something of a happy medium between the formal and the informal, providing structure to the interactions of people engaged in the shared pursuit of teaching. In the majority of cases, we have no way of exerting control over the way people interact (nor should we), although if we really want to change how education operates, we need to understand the forces involved.

It helps to return to what Dewey and Follett had to say about inquiry in groups. When a number of people have a stake in something, or are affected by the consequences of some activity, they often form groups in solidarity with one another to find new and better solutions to their problems. Such a group could be well organized, like the Highlander Folk School, where activists from around the country come together to learn new ways of mobilizing from one another, or it could be more informal, in the form of chats over coffee in the lunchroom that help people become acquainted with new ways of seeing.

This kind of dialogue raises an interesting point that we touched on briefly in the previous section. If teachers rely more on their instincts than on methods backed by empirical evidence, how many bad habits are they learning from peers? There is no straightforward way to tell, but it is easy to imagine that each new generation of teachers takes on the shortcomings of its predecessors. As mentioned previously, teachers carry models for their behaviour from their own student days, possibly reinforced by the community of teacher colleagues. The challenge here is to counter the perception that, when standard courses of action appear successful, they amount to good practices. Too often, pitfalls or adjustments remain in what Erving Goffman called the "backstage," and are neither seen nor discussed.[22] How often have you seen a teacher admit to struggling with the content or the pedagogy? Such an admission is perceived as almost unprofessional.

Of course, if bad habits are passed on, so too are good habits, and it would be a mistake to suggest a pedagogical slippery slope. Much of our knowledge about effective teaching is the result of an instructor somewhere hitting upon a good idea, which others then pick up and run with, although sometimes this means little more than giving credence to practices developed elsewhere. Informal learning, however, is both a blessing and a curse: a source of shady ideas as well as solid ones, depending on what practices and habits the group models.

Recent theorists have taken to calling the groups that organize around specific goals or professions "communities of practice,"[23] and have moved the discussion forward by showing that different communities of practice have different norms that give order to the way they function. Lawyers pass on the value of doing more or less extensive research to develop helpful case histories. Doctors are instilled with the responsibility to keep themselves up to date with contemporary medical knowledge. Taxi drivers bend traffic laws, within reason, to get their fares to their destinations more quickly. These norms are communicated to new members, who then make them part of their own *modus operandi*.

Although they evolve, community norms tend to emerge from prior training and experience. By changing the way we train teachers, we could make it possible to influence the way teachers approach their jobs. This could have a trickle-down influence over time as norms are reinforced when members of the community of practice interact. We do not propose a military-style process in which inductees undergo a complete resocialization process to gain membership status – this would be ridiculous for teachers. Instead, we should value the creativity and individuality of instructors. The knowledge each of us gathers about the situations we move through on a daily basis, as well as the expertise we develop at detecting and evaluating the social context, helps us to find better solutions to common problems.

Teachers do what they do because it seems to work best for them. If they are to change their perspective, they need to be convinced that there is a better alternative, and to discover it through inquiry. They need opportunities to gain field experience with empirically validated techniques and to engage in research themselves. This is what we mean by learning to teach.

The theory of experiential learning doubles back on itself. Not only do students learn best by working through and breaking down established habits, so too do teachers. We propose a teacher education program that balances the habitual repertoires of established educational programs, district curricula, and experienced teachers with a process of incorporating creative solutions. Learning and creativity come naturally in situations where typical approaches fail, which is why real world experiences are so valuable. Learning to be a professional teacher involves acquiring a set of routines for teaching that emphasizes interpreting a context and generating knowledge that can be incorporated into future contexts and new possibilities for action.

So, the challenge we face in reforming the education system is to shift the norms for teachers away from habit and towards creativity (or inquiry). Too often, we praise teachers for being good at their job or malign them for being bad, when at issue are training and socialized attitudes. Facilitating the kind of learning we call for here would demand collegiality and a more inclusive educational institution. The broad prescription for achieving that goal would emphasize a full dialogue among teachers, students, parents, and the community about the nature of education and its goals.

We might consider introducing new and pre-service teachers to the concept of communities of practice. In the broadest of brush strokes, and at the very least, the candidate could begin to wrestle with the flawed idea that learning is a special form of individual activity, somehow separated from everyday life. The view that learning is the prototypical human activity would prepare teachers to incorporate the full range of their experiences into learning experiences both in and out of the classroom.

Could We Win Teachers Over?

Teachers are constantly admonished to hone their craft. They go through training and certification programs to expose them to prevailing ideas, and they are expected to engage in lifelong learning that includes professional development. Over the past few decades, policy makers and researchers have provided various kinds of punishments and incentives to teachers, hoping to motivate them towards improving their practice. Most of these efforts have been only marginally successful. Although most teachers understand that lifelong learning is worthwhile, it has been apparent for nearly fifty years that they often rely more on instinct than on science in the classroom.[24]

We need to acknowledge this reality in proposing an evidence-based approach to the issue of educational reform, starting from the perspective of institutional design. An experimenting institution that incorporated state-of-the-art practices at a steady rate should maximize educational quality over time. Clearly teachers, as the primary practitioners, need to be on board. Since it seems that the profession has not yet made the shift to a more experimental stance, any institutional design hoping to move in that direction would need to make provisions for teacher training and retraining just to bring the profession in line with current knowledge about teaching and learning.

For inspiration we could turn to other professions that already operate under assumptions that mesh well with the premises of an evidence-based institution. In particular, interventionist practices such as medicine and psychiatry are founded on a commitment to deploy the best available science to address each situation and, as a consequence, require practitioners to keep abreast of the latest developments. Thus, when someone dealing with depression approaches his or her doctor or therapist for advice, the professional has various options to recommend, from cognitive behavioural therapy to antidepressants, each based on up-to-date empirical data. If new research were to show another therapeutic approach to be more effective, it would supplant less effective approaches as the predominant prescription.

If a more empirical ethos is to be introduced into education, something similar would have to develop within the profession of teaching. Math principles, for example, would be taught according to the best available scientific data, and instructors would adjust their approaches whenever new information came to light. Making such changes would require both rethinking existing training and certification programs and creating new programs to help established teachers adjust to new expectations. The former would be necessary to reproduce the values of research across the profession in each successive generation. The latter is an essential element of the intermediate stages of institutional reform: existing teachers cannot – and emphatically should not – be replaced by institutional design; they would be essential as core participants in the new regime and key determinants of its success.

Gaining the support of current teachers for the new institutional structure and professional expectations would demand careful attention, and they could be approached in multiple ways. To begin with, existing teachers would have to be assured that their voices are important and that they would have an impact on the ensuing revisions. Their life experiences contain both the frustration and the promise of contemporary education, and could point the way towards new avenues of inquiry. If an institution were to add up all the experiences of every teacher, it would create a matrix for cross-case analysis that indicated successful and unsuccessful interventions and the environment's prevailing circumstances. These data would multiply the power of an experimental institution to develop new theories and improve educational practices over time. We explore these ideas more fully in the next chapter.

It would be important to avoid peppering teachers with surveillance. Evaluation is an integral part of an experimental institution, but this applies mainly to the experimental arm, staffed by researchers and specialized teachers. For teachers in generic classrooms, evaluation should play much the same role as it does today, ensuring quality control without being overly intrusive. At the same time, it should be made clear that the institution would gradually increase demands on teachers in terms of professionalization, making education more of an applied science. This could be accomplished by transforming the norms of the profession and by incorporating basic accountability boards to deal with infractions, not by creating an onerous accountability structure inside the classroom.

Because the intermediate phases of reform would rely heavily on retaining and winning over existing teachers, it might also be important to emphasize that their day-to-day activities would not change dramatically. At the initial stage of the institutional rollout, not many experiments would have reached the point where standard practices and curriculum would have been revised to account for them. Although teachers would need to make some adjustments, in addition to keeping themselves informed about recommended methods and common issues, the newly reformed institution would still resemble its predecessor.

So far we have addressed only the primary service providers in education, but what about its users – students and their parents? The expectations and responsibilities of students and parents today, having been socialized into existing institutions over decades, are not entirely in step with an experimental institution. As the world becomes increasingly organized to minimize risk,[25] public experimentation sounds more and more counterintuitive – any value inherent to scientific experimentation seems to be overridden by the dangers associated with the unknown. In the previous section we sought to explain the need for institutional controls to balance the two, which would help allay concerns, but the public's perception of experimentation would need to shift for an institutional reform of this type to succeed. On its surface, this shift would require something like an information campaign during the initial stages of reform. Such a campaign would explain that experimentation in education depends on existing stores of knowledge, and that risk would be maintained in proportion to the confidence experts have in the premises underlying an application. Students and parents would also need to be made aware that most students would take part in only two or three experimental classrooms over the entire period of their education. Measured across their entire educational experience, students would experience net benefits in an experimental institution. We explore this issue in more detail later.

Although the transition might be difficult for portions of the population, there is already an established market for alternative education, indicating that some people would welcome the opportunity to engage in cutting-edge classrooms. People who enrol their children in private schools or home-schooling often do so out of mistrust of guiding ideologies (secularism versus religion, for instance) in mainstream education. But those who use alternative education because they believe that it offers higher educational quality might appreciate adaptive education's commitment to empirical data. The same might be said of people who believe certain forms of alternative education capture the nature of human psychology more closely than does mainstream education. We are confident that adaptive education, with its reliance on data, speaks to the concerns of this group.

6   The Role of the Epistemic Division

For the theories and hypotheticals that have occupied us for the bulk of this book to take shape in the real world and to have a measurable impact on the quality of teaching and learning in our schools, we envision an institutional add-on to existing school systems that would elicit, plan, and oversee research, analyse results, and ensure that those results find their way to front-line educators so that they can incorporate new knowledge into their practice. We have named this add-on the Epistemic Division, a term we feel reflects our commitment to increasing the knowledge base available to educators by encouraging the systematic collection of data and by recognizing the relative validity of knowledge gained from multiple sources and perspectives.

The aim of this chapter is to provide a thorough description of the Epistemic Division, its departments, and the process we propose for planning, implementing, analysing, and disseminating results of on-site research. To illustrate the potential and flexibility of this approach, we turn at the conclusion to three concrete examples of research projects originating from different sources and following different trajectories.

The Epistemic Division

Governance of the Epistemic Division might well vary from jurisdiction to jurisdiction, sometimes coming under the administration of local or regional school boards, sometimes administered jointly with local universities, and sometimes having a provincial/state or even national organizational structure. Of course, no one starts from scratch when designing new institutions or adding new structures to existing ones, so we expect the Epistemic Division would make use of whatever internal infrastructure and resources exist within the current educational system to buttress its efforts. We can also see ways in which it could link with external institutions to their mutual benefit, sharing key functions, infrastructure, or human resources.

Although the governance and institutional structures might vary, the essential focus – as we have indicated in previous chapters – would be on local actors carrying out locally generated projects involving novel pedagogies, various institutional arrangements, and everyday practices. In addition to these locally generated projects, the adaptive education model would also support mandated themes put forward by policy makers to address specific areas of concern – say, environmental education or playground bullying. These themes would originate from a central government department or ministry, and become priority research topics within the Epistemic Division.

Regardless of the proposal's origin, it would be the responsibility of the Epistemic Division to determine what projects are worth pursuing, what risks are involved, and how those risks balance confidence in the anticipated outcomes, and to develop a research design. When initial data are available for analysis, it would also be the Division's responsibility to decide whether the project should be scaled up, scaled down, or abandoned. And ultimately the Division would be responsible for disseminating the knowledge gained, along with recommendations for practical application and follow-up research.

To carry out these core functions, we envision three departments functioning within the Epistemic Division: the Implementation Department, the Analysis Department, and the Knowledge Department. As illustrated in Figure 1, each department would consist of teams of experts and committees who would ensure that decisions and plans were made with the best possible information in hand. Although the following descriptions summarize their roles within the Epistemic Division, the lines separating these departments frequently would blur as data analysts made recommendations about project design or knowledge experts consulted with the Implementation Department in preparing public reports. This interaction will become clear in the detailed examples that conclude this chapter.

The Implementation Department

The Implementation Department would be responsible for producing a well-designed research project and carrying it to conclusion. It would

Figure 1 The Organization of the Epistemic Division

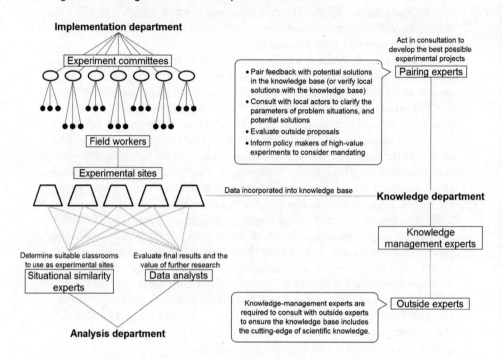

form an Experiment Committee, specific to each project, featuring local and expert knowledge as well as representatives from the other two departments. The committee, under the leadership of a project manager, would oversee the project from its initial design through data collection and would be responsible for the integrity of the data-collection process.

As indicated in Figure 1, the Implementation Department would also be responsible for training and monitoring fieldworkers to ensure that data were collected in strict adherence to the research design.

The Implementation Department would also undertake outreach programs to build the community support necessary to maintain the numerous partnerships and other supports on which it would rely to get research proposals off the ground.

Permanent members of the Implementation Department would include *project management experts*, who would initiate projects in diverse settings, with disparate stakeholders with various agendas;

methodologists, who would operationalize and monitor research design; and *substantive content experts*, who would contribute knowledge, research experience, and expertise in several major areas of education, such as pedagogy, curriculum, learning, social justice, special education, teacher education, and learning assessment.

The Analysis Department

As its name implies, the Analysis Department would analyse and evaluate the data collected by fieldworkers in various research projects. Adjudicating the success of an experiment – based on knowledge generation as much as on final results – would be an especially important function in the adaptive education model. The adjudication would lead to decisions about whether or not the experiment should be tried again, scaled up, or dropped. Data analysts would make this determination by undertaking a risk analysis and evaluating the level of confidence in the initial findings.

In doing its work, the Analysis Department typically would gather a diverse body of data and cutting-edge research, relying in part on the latest educational literature housed in the Knowledge Department's large repository.

Two teams of experts, *situational similarity experts* and *data analysts* – primarily statisticians and qualitative data analysts – would form the core of the Analysis Department. It would be the role of the situational similarity team to select the pilot setting for the first run of a project or, in situations where multiple research sites were necessary, to find numerous classrooms that had the necessary contextual criteria. If a decision were made to scale up the pilot research project, the situational similarity experts would need to produce relevant criteria for selecting future research sites.

In a task unusual for statisticians, the data analysts in this department would be expected to apply expansive notions of success that prioritize knowledge generation. They would also be responsible for the publication of a final report in various formats that reflected the Epistemic Division's commitment to dissemination.

The Knowledge Department

The Knowledge Department would elicit, evaluate, and approve proposals, operate a database of relevant research, engage in outreach, and help incorporate successful innovations into standard practice through a process we call "normatization."

The department would consist of *pairing experts*, who would seek to develop the best possible research projects by linking problems identified in the community with expert insights and relevant knowledge, and *knowledge management experts*, who would disseminate research, primarily using the repository of relevant literature and final reports of the research projects.

Research proposals would be the lifeblood of the adaptive education institution, and their first stop would be here, in the Knowledge Department. Led by pairing experts, the department would host information and outreach sessions to introduce teachers and community members to the concept of adaptive education, encourage an interest in evidence-based education, and solicit specific suggestions for research projects. Next, a Review Board led by pairing experts and including permanent members of the Epistemic Division and outside experts would adjudicate proposals to determine if they merited further consideration. The Review Board would also be responsible for honing the research design. When these steps neared completion and if reviews were favourable, the Implementation Department would form its Experiment Committee.

The kind of information required for adjudicating research proposals and providing feedback would be readily available in the department's user-friendly educational library and database of broad-based and peer-reviewed educational literature. This repository, created and maintained by knowledge management experts, would also store documentation of the Epistemic Division's various experiments, including ongoing projects and an accessible version of a Handbook of Best Practices in Education. Information from the repository would be made available as a public service, providing statistical and other evidence on educational research and helping users distinguish reality from media hype.

As a part of its outreach mandate, the Knowledge Department would also be responsible for building a communication plan that included regular research updates and invitations to practising teachers to participate in research. Citizen researchers or public intellectuals could attend these sessions and enter into dialogue with teachers and administrators about potential areas of research, help prepare a proposal, or participate in a research project.

As a final step in the process that would begin here with a local problem or an individual idea, the Knowledge Department would also be responsible for normatization – the standardization and dissemination of best practices. Indeed, this is the *raison d'être* of adaptive education: the introduction of evidence-based practice into classrooms.

As successive runs of a specific experiment moved innovative ideas for solving an educational problem closer to acceptance as best practice, knowledge management experts would ensure that its results were disseminated in relevant curricula, teacher-training modules, and professional development workshops. Knowledge management experts might produce and publish a journal article on a specific project, co-authored by researchers, teachers, and community members. Ultimately, the Knowledge Department might publish its own journal.

The desired result of adaptive education is collaboration across organizations, sectors, and institutions, fostering an increased institutional capacity for research and reform. The Knowledge Department would be central to this effort as the endpoint of a process to identify evidence-based solutions to thoroughly researched problems.

The trajectory of a project

Although both Figure 1 and the descriptions above suggest a linear progression from the initial idea through the implementation of a project, data collection and analysis, and ultimate dissemination of results, in fact the arrangement would be far more interconnected. The primary responsibility for idea generation would lie with the Knowledge Department, but the Implementation Department – as the group responsible for undertaking the research – would participate in those decisions. During the implementation process, the Analysis Department would provide regular input. Data analysis necessarily involves decisions about how to proceed and whether to add sites or sift target populations, and these decisions would depend on input from the Implementation Department as well as access to relevant existing data from the Knowledge Department. The model would be intentionally fluid to encourage the creative engagement of participants from a variety of perspectives.

That being said, we have tried to capture the process in Figure 2. Reading the figure horizontally, the middle portion portrays the overall process. The different phases are labelled, and move from idea generation to normatization. The figure also highlights the important feedback loops that would be initiated in the evaluation and

Figure 2 The Process of Adaptive Education

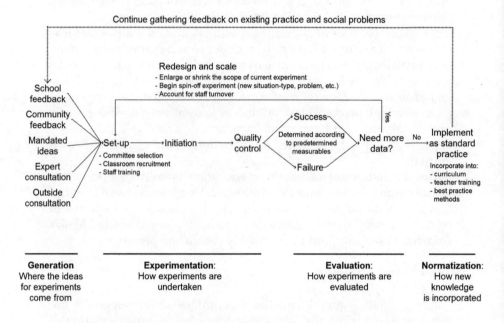

Generation	Experimentation:	Evaluation:	Normatization:
Where the ideas for experiments come from	How experiments are undertaken	How experiments are evaluated	How new knowledge is incorporated

normatization phases and the return to the experimentation and idea phases, respectively.

The following three examples of very different projects illustrate more concretely how we see this model playing out in the messy world of real people in real educational environments.

MATH PRECONCEPTIONS, DRAMATIC NARRATIVES, AND LEARNING
Our first example from an imaginary adaptive education institution explores the secondary context and features an intervention in math education that uses drama to increase student outcomes. The idea comes from a new teacher who garners additional support for three reasons. First, her solution quickly finds a constituency among her colleagues. Second, dramatic fantasy themes in text and television have become extremely popular among her students. Third, the existing literature helps ground the proposal in the research.

The proposal. The teacher's proposal is to apply Dorothy Heathcote's "pedagogy of the mantle of the expert" to a grade 10 high school math course.[1] The aim of the mantle of the expert is to use stories and other props to invest students emotionally in dramatic roles associated with a hypothetical scenario in the subject area discipline – in this case, math. According to the mantle hypothesis, belief in and empathy for these "as if" situations will encourage learners to care about the math curriculum that is central to the drama. The inspiration for this proposal comes from Susan Gerofsky's research on the use of Heathcote's drama-in-education in several mathematical settings.[2]

The teacher who proposes the idea has attempted the drama-in-education pedagogy, and what she notices hints at this method's potential. At a weekly in-service professional development meeting, she approaches the principal and other teachers in the school with her idea. Every teacher/school participant acknowledges the school's disappointing math performance in standard exams. The principal approaches the parent-teacher group and the school board for funds to develop a grant proposal, and the money is used to hire a professional grant writer who prepares an initial proposal for a pilot research project. The methods section of the proposal recommends the use of school grades as an outcome to be investigated, using the rationale that the previous year's grades can be compared with the forthcoming year's grades, as these records are retained.

The response. The Review Board recommends the proposal for funding. In supporting this decision, the pairing experts draw upon the Knowledge Department's repository of peer-reviewed articles and practitioner experiences, focusing on the pedagogy of drama-in-education. As a result of the literature review, pairing experts concur with both the interpretation of the original concern and the possible solution of drama-in-math-education; however, they recommend a simple pre- and post-intervention that uses a survey tool to ask the grade 10 students about their perceptions of math as well as plans for future courses in math and statistics. This additional information will enable the researchers to make inferences, albeit imperfect ones, about possible long-term outcomes of the pedagogy. It should be noted that the reviewers – researchers themselves, some with extensive experience in classroom data collection and analysis – are not daunted by the proposed experiment's relatively radical intervention or its several disciplinary dimensions (math, drama, set design, and so on).

Because the literature review suggested the positive effects in math performance with some possible differences in performance due to gender and socio-economic factors, the Review Board agrees on an initial run of five classrooms in one school district, featuring significant differences in socio-economic status and including both an all-male and an all-female private school.

The following dramatic performance is created as an intervention in a math class. It consists of scenarios that are quite similar to those developed by Gerofsky, but it takes into account several trends in local youth culture. The first is the contemporary fascination of many fifteen-year-olds with fantasy novels and reality television. The second is vivid accounts in the news and elsewhere of child soldiers conscripted into armies to protect their families from the threat of violence. The third, based largely on anecdotal evidence, is the perception that students have a growing disinterest in the political process. This mixture of enabling and disempowering contexts is incorporated to create greater resonance in the scenario.

In the first scenario, entitled "Survivors and Saviours," high school students are characters in an action-novel-like setting where their expertise is needed to save their home city. Teachers and students both play roles in this drama: teachers represent the resistance movement, while students adopt pseudonyms and personal histories that suggest mathematical expertise. In the narrative, the students have hidden their expertise to avoid detection by the enemy. Their roles as cryptographers, logisticians, network theorists, and computer programmers introduce the necessary mathematical dimension to the program. The students are told that their efforts are needed to break enemy code, determine the flight trajectories of rockets and drones, hack the web for enemy communications, and gather military intelligence on weaponry. Resistance members (teachers) attempt to recruit the mathematicians in this hypothetical scenario. The young mathematicians are recruited willingly, and are ultimately taken away to "centres" to work at undermining enemy forces. These cave-like centres contain rudimentary resources such as pencils, paper, tablets, and solar calculators. The mathematicians soon forget the manner in which they were brought to the centres, and become engulfed in both the work and the greater cause of the resistance. The proposal attempts to use this hypothetical situation as a vehicle to excite students about what mathematicians can do.

The implementation. The Experiment Committee, which oversees all five schools in this inaugural test of the idea, includes a project manager with experience at maintaining multiple sites of operation, a curriculum design expert from the Knowledge Department with a background in drama, the original teacher and principal, the heads of the math departments at the four other schools, and a math education professor from a local university. The university supports the overall experiment by providing space and some resources for the Implementation Department. The university professor on the committee runs a course with a community service-learning component, and some of his students become fieldworkers for the project.

To maximize the quality of data collection, a situational similarity expert works closely with a small number of fieldworkers to ensure that a carefully crafted partial script is followed to guard against salient differences among them. (Research in the dramatic arts reveals that fully developed scripts reduce the level of engagement.) The partial script builds a scenario by delineating the physical setting and describing roles. The fieldworkers, who are trained in this technique and who can assist in the training sessions created for the Implementation Department, also deliver the pre- and post-surveys. Indeed, if done properly, this training will facilitate positive feelings about the local experiment model and build a stronger research team.

Data analysts create a baseline for the research based on grades from the previous five years and the pre-survey. All of the data will be used to evaluate the pedagogy and any differences in its effectiveness when controlling for gender and socio-economic status. Despite the obvious insights they might bring, no video or observations will be collected, as the fieldwork and related literature have found them to be disruptive. Situational similarity experts will contribute contextual data to provide important background in the final report and to generate criteria for finding other classrooms should the first run justify the project's continuation.

Analysing the data. The final report finds significant differences in math performance between classrooms using drama-in-math-education and classrooms in previous years that did not. Moreover, the survey data indicate that, after the intervention, students have greater interest in and respect for math. The experts in the Analysis Department remain supportive of the idea, and in the lessons learned/recommendations section of the final report they call for a second run of fifteen classrooms. They also recommend that the scope be altered so that the idea can be tested across different grade levels. This reconfiguration is due to concerns regarding the widespread applicability of the pedagogy. Until this point, the research literature has focused only on grade 10 students.

The Experiment Committee's support of this expansion of the study is based largely on its confidence in both the pedagogy and the original study. There is some turnover in the teachers and fieldworkers for the second run, largely due to the expectation of increased time commitments and to pre-service teachers finding their first jobs in education.

Next steps. The Knowledge Department recommends the collection of enrolment data for all elective math courses across the district, to see if there is a surge in popularity in math after this method is employed. When the second run finishes, data analysts find significant positive results across every grade in both student performance and intentions to pursue math courses in the future. As suspected, enrolment in elective math courses has increased across the district following the district-wide implementation.

The specific findings are noteworthy because they detail how the Epistemic Division of the adaptive education institution can make a positive contribution to possible educational policy. One aspect of the data analysis broke the students into quintiles based on the previous year's grades. Upon examination, the lowest quintile was responsible for nearly 40 per cent of the improvement. These same students were then tracked for their open-ended comments on their perceptions of math in the survey instrument. The comments from the lowest-quintile students were remarkably similar in their newfound interpretation of math as a collective, rather than an individual, experience. As one student hypothetically writes, "Before, I saw math as a way for the teacher to show the others in the class how dumb I was. Since it has become about groups and acting, I know I can ask others for help, and they are friendly and helpful." A specialist in low achievers explains that the drama classroom is a non-threatening form of intervention and creates a more cohesive classroom. The introduction of drama is similar to a special education class for those struggling in math, but different in that stigma and anxiety are largely removed.

Publication of the data leads to two long-term impacts. The first is methodological: the Knowledge Department requires all subsequent data collection and analysis to include and maintain data on lower-achieving students. The second arises indirectly from a recently completed cross-cultural study analysing the occupational opportunities for lower-quintile students in countries with high levels of social cohesion. The findings not only link increased career opportunities to high social cohesion; they also identify education as the most likely factor in its cultivation. Several governments concerned about social cohesion designate specific funding to support lower-quintile students, and social cohesion becomes a key concept in policy circles for a number of years following this experiment.

Normatization. A third run of the drama-in-math experiment is designed to double-check results before committing it to normatization. Data analysts determine that forty-five classrooms spread across the country should be employed, with various combinations of math subjects and grade levels. The goals are to confirm the experimental data already gleaned and to investigate their broader application. Many schools volunteer to be part of the next run, but classrooms are chosen using criteria established by the situational similarity experts, using a recruitment process that includes a professional development workshop at a national conference of math educators. Recent media attention typically has focused on improved performance, but in some cases it has questioned the pedagogy. In response, the Knowledge Management group generates a working paper on the history of the "mantle of the expert" pedagogy and its application in this context.

The success of this innovation leads policy makers and politicians to ask the Knowledge Department to redeploy the project in an effort to apply the model to other disciplines, such as chemistry. This split-off project will occur simultaneously with the third run. This mandated idea does not need approval, and is justified because of the emerging popularity and relevance of STEM (science, technology, engineering, and mathematics).[3]

Normatization occurs without qualification. Math teachers in training become well acquainted with this pedagogy by drawing upon the series of reports and published papers on the experiment. The reports are written in an efficient and accessible manner, picking up where earlier ones left off. The repository contains the project reports, augmented by other relevant material using its data-storage capabilities. Users can also mine the data using keywords to combine elements that were not studied in the specific experiment (for example, history education and drama). Professional development seminars on this pedagogy are made available to existing teachers of math and science and to those from other disciplines who might be interested.

Curriculum designers are apprised of the normatization status, and a partial script and lesson plan from one of the classes are attached to a memo encouraging any jurisdiction that is revising its math curricula to feature learning objectives that align with the pedagogy. A professional association of math and science educators creates a special interest group that builds on the lessons learned in the initial runs of this experiment in order to strengthen the feasibility of the pedagogy.

Summing up. In this example, drama-in-math-education proved to be a creative solution to a habitual negative response to math among some students. It showed how the Epistemic Division model encourages the kind of expansive thinking that allows creative ideas to find their way into educational practice. The data analysts' decision to gather findings across a host of diverse settings instilled quick confidence in the new pedagogy, and their early identification of the impact on low achievers allowed them to add another layer of significance to the data. This example also highlights the normatization process and the efforts to disseminate a newly identified best practice.

DELOCALIZED STUDENTS: ITUNES FOR INTRODUCTORY ENGLISH

The proposal. University officials approach the Epistemic Division with a proposal to offer a course with both an in-person and an online enrolment option. The setting is a mandatory introductory English course with six hundred students – call it "English 101: Reading and Writing about Literature." Three hundred students will participate in a traditional, face-to-face class with the instructor, while another three hundred delocalized students will "attend" the same lectures remotely. This delocalized format differs from an online course in that it does not support asynchronous engagement with course content. Delocalized students can be off-campus, but they must attend the lecture virtually at the same time as it is physically offered; the lectures are essentially live-streamed. The instructor grades attendance and polls both the face-to-face and online students at various times during the lecture to arrive at a participation grade.

The university officials present a fourfold rationale to the Knowledge Department. In attempting to cultivate a niche, the post-secondary university in this example – call it Dumdorf University – has made it a priority to increase enrolment by recruiting both high school graduates from the host region and mature, lifelong learners. In this context, officials argue, delocalized classrooms would decrease the growing dependency of the university on large lecture halls. Only three such spaces currently exist at Dumdorf, demand is high, and no new buildings are being erected. They also argue that delocalized classrooms would provide additional flexibility in scheduling classes, ease the traffic burden on campus, and allow the university to develop the tools to serve the needs of a more diverse student population.

They have chosen English 101 as the subject pool for this delocalized experiment because of its status as a mandatory course for all incoming students. In addition, the percentage of English majors in each of the sections is historically low, which limits possible harm to the English Department caused by any negative results of the experiment. The department has experienced and confident instructors with few qualms about experiments involving large numbers, since large course sizes are the norm in introductory English offerings. Finally, from a research perspective the number of subjects will make it easier to generate statistically robust results.

Dumdorf officials propose that, for the initial experiment, three sections of the course will be conducted via video, message-enabled, voice-over-Internet-Protocol technology such as Skype, and managed through an innovative program similar to iTunes. Nine teaching assistants will support each of the three instructors (and double as Implementation Department fieldworkers). The university proposes to compare learning outcomes of students who attend face-to-face lectures and those who are enrolled in the delocalized alternative. Its research question asks if the alternative can feasibly complement or even replace traditional classrooms, using a typical grade distribution as the baseline and student grades as the measure of success.

The response. When it receives this request, the Knowledge Department immediately expresses two concerns. First, the idea is emerging from an unconventional pathway for idea generation, mainly because universities are neither the typical experts nor local actors in the Epistemic Division model. Second, the idea, if not the research, is fraught with political implications. Because it would apply only to the post-secondary landscape – where every campus is experimenting with hybrid courses – and because the university could take it up single-handedly if the proposed digital format is shown to be an inexpensive form of education, the university might be seen as an unfair benefactor. To address these concerns, the Review Board seeks input from a provincial ministry of higher education. The ministry recommends categorizing the proposal as a mandated theme, giving it a leg-up in the adaptive education process.

Despite their qualms, the knowledge management experts assigned to the case recognize that this idea has cutting-edge implications and sufficient theoretical grounding in distance education to warrant investigation. They point to one journal's recent volume, which explored the social impacts of distance education in terms of access, as well as its other merits, such as cost efficiency. However, previous research on delocalized classrooms did not gather comparative data on student performance. Taking into account the perspectives of both the ministry and the knowledge management experts, pairing experts assemble a special Review Board for this proposal consisting of distance educators, technologists, situational similarity experts, data analysts, and one high-ranking official from the ministry.

The Review Board approves the project, but recommends only limited funding because, in the view of the pairing experts, the university's classrooms are already large and efficient. This seemingly tight-fisted response also reflects some lingering scepticism about the idea and its motivations. For its part, the university will house the project and pay for the three instructors and the teaching assistants/fieldworkers. The focus will be on the performance and satisfaction of the delocalized portion of the introductory English classroom.

The implementation. Initially, the Experiment Committee assembled by the Implementation Department is identical to the specially formulated Review Board except for the addition of a pairing expert from the Knowledge Department to serve as project manager. This person is an experienced administrator, and she establishes an implementation plan that focuses largely on quality control concerns. For example, the use of three sections with different instructors is an obvious concern because differences in teaching style might affect the reliability of the comparison. The project manager is also concerned about the possible negative effect on the overall quality of instruction and the ethics of involving industry in the provision the technology.[4] For these reasons, she adds another permanent member of the Implementation Department to the Experiment Committee. This person is an expert methodologist who oversees the teaching assistants/fieldworkers responsible for monitoring the lectures and technology, looking for discrepancies among the three curricula, their instruction, and their electronic delivery. As a group of educators, the Experiment Committee is also particularly interested in the principles of learning that are guiding the use of the technology.

The research design of the original proposal sought to determine whether the distribution of student performance for those enrolled in the delocalized portion of the section (three hundred students across three sections) would indicate an experimental effect – for example, would the percentage of students in the B range change in the delocalized version? A straightforward statistical analysis shows that students' historical performance over the past several years has been similar. The Experiment Committee expects the experimental sample to be comparable. The Review Board and pairing experts recommend a student satisfaction survey be used to collect further data.

The Experiment Committee offers a training seminar to introduce instructors and teaching assistants/fieldworkers to the research design, technology, data collection, and content-and-delivery method for each lesson. The lesson plans generally feature a twenty-minute lecture followed by questions and answers.[5] The question-and-answer segment of the lesson plan is designed primarily to empower students to ask questions. This is an intentionally straightforward pedagogical approach that encourages the active engagement of students and diminishes differences among the three instructors that might occur with various other pedagogies. Addressing issues of content and student comprehension, the Experiment Committee decides that instructors will attend to the three hundred students in front of them, while two teaching assistants/fieldworkers track the online engagement of the other three hundred students. The teaching assistants/fieldworkers log and alert the instructor to the presence of online questions.

Industry personnel on the Experiment Committee manage the technological aspects and explain troubleshooting strategies. The company's servers also support the course with plenty of bandwidth. As a result, the focus of the training relates to navigational issues and the incorporation of slideshows, additional URLs, and guest speakers in both the online and face-to-face content. Teaching assistants/fieldworkers are also able to troubleshoot minor glitches in the technology, handle data collection, and deliver the student satisfaction survey electronically.

Analysing the data. Formative evaluation includes the use of the university's standard student satisfaction survey at the six-week and twenty-six-week marks of the two-term course. The survey instrument contains quantitative and qualitative questions – the latter an open-ended question about desired changes. The survey is scheduled to coincide with mid-term and end-of-term course requirements that provide data on grade distribution, with a summative evaluation tool to be delivered at the end of the second term. Survey data on satisfaction will be collected from the instructors as well.

A cursory analysis of the qualitative elements of the mid-term student satisfaction survey leads data analysts to investigate user data patterns in more detail. They discover that, although the delocalized students signed into the live lectures, there was very little chatting or emailing during the lectures in the first few weeks. This is not an issue for the in-person portion of the course, as each instructor elicited an average of eight to eleven questions or comments during each lecture. In other words, delocalized students might sign in, but they do not engage. One teaching assistant/fieldworker hypothesizes that this is a case of self-selection bias; those students who choose the delocalized option might do so because they want to avoid the participation component that is inherent in face-to-face attendance. Educational research is clear that student engagement is positively correlated with grades, making this discovery problematic for the project.

After a joint meeting of the Experiment Committee, representatives of the Analysis Department perform a quick but thorough examination of the quantitative portion of the satisfaction survey. The analysis of the survey does not detect dissatisfaction among either population. As a result, an on-the-fly adjustment requiring delocalized students to ask questions regarding the lecture is implemented across all three sections. Ultimately, this adjustment is effective in promoting the minimum participation levels necessary to compare the delocalized students with the face-to-face students. The instructors' evaluations, however, might be at risk for two reasons. First, changing course requirements midstream is generally not good policy. Second and related, the increased emphasis on delocalized students' engagement has the unintended consequence of reducing in-person student questions and comments. These risks, shouldered by the instructors but potentially harmful to both the instructors and the students, are an excellent example of the tension between the risks and benefits of this model.

The remainder of the academic year goes smoothly. Data analysts report that the proportion of high grades (A and B+) remain comparable in both versions of the course. In other words, good students in both the delocalized and face-to-face environments can transcend any challenges the research might have introduced. However, grades of B, B–, and C+ found in the typical grade distribution become C, C–, and D in the delocalized environment, which suggests the distinct possibility that some students are affected detrimentally by not attending live lectures. Analysts hypothesize that the usual inhabitants of this grade range lack motivation in the delocalized setting.

The Analysis Department's final report judges the delocalized intervention itself a failure because of the sharp drop-off in the grades of delocalized students. This does not mean that the research itself is a failure, as it has furthered knowledge about hybrid classrooms. Indeed, the data analysts acknowledge that student satisfaction is surprisingly strong even among delocalized students, which, after careful inquiry and discussion, they attribute to an interest in using a technology that provides an alternative to the traditional lecture hall. The instructors are supportive, too, except that they believe they should be awarded a greater number of teaching credits for such large classes. In the end, however, the ethical quandary posed by using an enticing technology that ultimately might disaffect already-disadvantaged students is key to the decision not to renew the proposal.

Next steps. From the perspective of adaptive education, projects featuring face-to-face and delocalized students remain in abeyance for three years because of the failed innovation. Eventually, a proposal for redeployment of this experiment comes at the behest of one of the original instructors, who has continued to experiment on her own with some versions of this model in upper-level classes and in partnership with the technology company. The new proposal explains that third- and fourth-year students are better subjects for the research because they are more confident and knowledgeable about the discipline, and more willing to engage with the rest of the class. Pragmatically speaking, the university's English Department has also decided that first-year courses are the source of English majors and worth the additional investment in smaller, more numerous sections.[6] The instructor's own follow-up outcomes – namely, equitable student grade distribution and individual student satisfaction – are included in the proposal.

This second proposal is admittedly modest, but it lacks the learning principles and theory that were problematic in the first run. The knowledge management experts and the Review Board recategorize the proposal as a pilot study. They argue that it aligns with a different proposal that addresses place-based learning possibilities, and they convince the authors to concentrate on studying strategies to engage delocalized students, instead of focusing on the technology itself. Among other things, place-based learning theory calls for the enlistment of numerous modalities, such as sound and smell, to enhance student engagement and understanding. The proposal, then, is to require delocalized students to beam images into the classroom from locations that resonate with various geographical and temporal elements of the literature being discussed. For example, early chapters in Michael Ondaatje's *In the Skin of Lion* will be discussed with students who are contributing their views while sitting on or near various pieces of urban infrastructure, such as a bridge. This revamped proposal also links the proposed study with three additional classrooms across several universities. The research would be pilot-like, sharing the results of a common course evaluation developed jointly as the primary evaluation tool.

The data analysts judge the pilot study a success because there is no drop off in the grades of delocalized students. The final report supports the use of place-based learning in an undergraduate English course, and analysts speculate that cross-fertilization among instructors is responsible for the high level of student satisfaction with the curriculum. On the negative side, the company responsible for the technology backs away from a subsequent proposal because it runs out of funding for the technology. The final report on the pilot study is entered into the database, and can be easily found using a search of place-based learning in an interdisciplinary context, as well as key terms such as technology, delocalized, comparative research, and hybrid classroom.

In retrospect the apparent failure of the original study could have been a result of timing. Coincidentally the double major route for undergraduates has grown rapidly. Departments that tend to be linked by students (for example, political science and international development) have responded with programs that stretch across one another. Modestly sized universities are linking their departments with other universities. One collaborative effort involves four schools that have created a cultural studies program linking sociology, ethnic studies, women's studies, and popular culture. They are now seeking technology similar to that used in the original study to facilitate the sharing of courses in ways that would enable participating students to learn more about other schools, cities, and even countries. Had the technology used in the original experiment been available, astute educational administrators at these smaller institutions would have supported its use in the courses that make up these new programs.

Summing up. This hypothetical experiment was intended to take the adaptive education institution into the realm of post-secondary education, where adaptation and flexibility in programming are key and growing considerations. The stakeholders included industry and technology, two powerful forces in education. The example accentuated the host of moving parts that might be involved in both the research and the on-the-fly nature of necessary changes. Researchers included professors, administrators, corporations, graduate students, and several representatives from the Epistemic Division of the larger institution. Various points of convergence among the researchers in this example might suggest the positive nature of collaboration within the model.

The idea originally sought to address administrative concerns, and evolved to produce a research project examining trends in post-secondary pedagogy and programming that emphasize technology and responsiveness. Important social considerations, such as the growing need to accommodate non-traditional post-secondary students, were factors. The example emphasized the Review Board's composition in light of the involvement of local expertise and industry. The story then became one of methodological difficulties, mixed findings, and a decrease in the scale of experimentation until, in the end, the study was discontinued.

COMMUNITY SERVICE LEARNING FOR ENVIRONMENTAL EDUCATION
This example addresses the community-based problem of the destruction of fish habitat on school grounds. The research project studies the use of community service learning (CSL) – a promising pedagogy that requires students to volunteer in community projects and to reflect upon the concepts they encounter there when they return to class – to promote behavioural change, and emphasizes local knowledge shared by a community-based organization, which adds expertise and credibility to the project. The example also highlights the proposed review process and the Experiment Committee's efforts at training and quality control, and the way data analysis can lead to new directions over successive runs.

The proposal. At a public meeting, called by the Knowledge Department to elicit and generate ideas for local experiments, volunteers for the Streamers, a community-based organization committed to the day-lighting of streams – the process of restoring a stream to its natural state after it has been covered over or replaced by culverts – and the protection of riparian zones, expresses concerns about the degradation of fish habitat in a stream that runs through a local schoolyard. The Streamers are concerned about children playing in the stream and disposing of waste in it. Erosion is destroying the habitat of existing animals, and the Streamers are concerned that continued destruction would discourage spawning fish from returning. The schoolyard is small – in fact, the recent daylighting of the stream that cuts across it has created the equivalent of a new children's playing surface, and the students use it in a variety of ways during recess. The discovery of a frog or a minnow, for example, leads to large numbers of students gathering on the embankment. The Streamers fear that the success of the daylighting – measured in terms of returning fish –will be compromised by the destruction of the riparian zone.

After the meeting, members of the organization approach the school principal with both their concerns and a partial solution, including an experimental classroom and the use of grade 7 students to perform community service by acting as stream monitors during recess and encouraging other students to stay out of the stream and off its banks. Together the school and the Streamers submit a proposal to the Knowledge Department,   .

In this example, environmental education is a provincially mandated theme, so the proposal for an environmental protection study follows a variation of the usual process and criteria for approval.[7] Since mandated themes might remain priorities for several years, many proposals involving numerous classrooms potentially could yield volumes of data, making it possible to compare the merits of each proposal upon completion of a single run. In this way, themes can become efficient levers for addressing a general area of concern using the Epistemic Division model. For example, in focusing on an environmental education theme, numerous experiments – including the one proposed here – might allow data analysts to compare CSL to other environmental education pedagogies or, in future runs, to use CSL in classrooms with different features (rural, K-3, low parental engagement, or low socio-economic status).

The elementary (K-7) school in this proposal is located in a relatively affluent neighbourhood where parental involvement is strong and the experienced school staff has a strong culture of leadership that includes running out-of-school programs, coaching athletic teams, and serving on school committees.

The response. A Review Board created specially to adjudicate proposals coming in via the environmental education theme supports the proposal with some modifications. Along with permanent members of the Epistemic Division, the Review Board comprises a public education expert, a member of a nationally recognized environmental non-governmental organization, and a local business representative.[8] In reviewing and ultimately accepting the proposal, the Review Board recommends the use of CSL pedagogy to achieve the project and curricular objectives.

In assembling the Experiment Committee, the project manager recognizes the need for extensive community representation to address potential concerns about any loss of community control. He includes a city planner on the committee, along with members of the Streamers. Membership in the committee allows the community organizations to maintain direct contact with the consenting grade 7 students, who are important school liaisons. Other members of the committee include a husband-and-wife research team from the United Kingdom, who bring extensive experience in co-researching local environmental issues with youth and who are well positioned to spearhead the methodology and offer ethical advice. Situational similarity experts also contribute to the Experiment Committee; they have a special interest in data collection and in the context of this experiment.

The proposal states the problem clearly, but the use of students as stream monitors receives a less enthusiastic response from the Experiment Committee. Although the work of the UK researchers asserts the need to make students more aware of research that focuses on them and to allow them to contribute to the development of the research instruments, in this case they caution against direct student involvement in monitoring and data collection, fearing it might arouse controversy in the community. Instead they argue for the use of pre-service teachers as fieldworkers.

Another major concern of the Experiment Committee is the absence of an associated school curriculum. To date, no effort has been made to connect the preservation of the stream to ministry-prescribed learning outcomes for any of the elementary grades. As a result of this concern, a second objective is introduced to the proposal: to improve children's attitudes and behaviour towards the stream through curricular content.[9] Teachers identified the grade 7 social studies curriculum – particularly its concept of citizenship education – as the likely source of this connection. One unit calls for community service learning that typically runs parallel to a buddy program, wherein older students are models and mentors to students in the earlier grades.

Under the revised proposal, still using a CSL model, the grade 7 students would work with the Streamers, municipal planners, and school board officials to protect the stream's natural spawning habitat. Their community service is, at one level, service to the school community, but at another level it is service to the city and natural world. In this way the goals of the CSL project are social in orientation (protection of the environment, service to the community) and adhere to the grade 7 social studies curriculum, which, among things, asks students to consider the duties of citizens in the protection of the non-human world. The teacher is able to formulate some guiding belief statements – for example, picking up trash when you encounter it is a citizen's responsibility – that will be examined in relation to the stream. Based on these statements, the teacher will invite the Streamers and other stakeholders to discuss the stream's habitat and their motivations for protecting it. Students will examine possible answers, then work collaboratively on signage or other efforts to discourage students from entering the stream. The revised proposal for research is sent to the Implementation Department.

The implementation. The CSL model requires volunteer students to collaborate with the Streamers, municipal planners, and school board officials on measures – such as building a pedestrian bridge, creating signage – designed to protect the stream. The teacher grades his students' learning gains in social studies through CSL-related course requirements (student logbooks and reflections). A graduate student studying CSL pedagogy supports the CSL portion of the social studies class by providing assistance to both the teacher and the students. Later, the graduate student's thesis will help inform the department or committee that evaluates these findings.

The primary unit of analysis is behavioural change among students, including learning gains in social studies, but the research design also provides for the evaluation of stakeholders, including community members and social studies teachers, based on the recognition that findings related to their participation will be particularly important in the first run of the project.[10]

Analysing the data. The Final Report deems the first run of this project a moderate success. The "real-life" nature of CSL appears to have produced accounts by grade 7 students indicating a desire to be good environmental citizens, thereby suggesting some support for the pedagogy. A combination of ongoing identification of environmental education as a ministry priority, favourable press coverage, and national census data revealing an appetite among parents for specialty schools using an environmental theme leads to a partial redeployment, despite the lack of a statistically significant change in student learning.

Next steps. The second run recruits four grade 7 classrooms to study behavioural change in a science class using the CSL pedagogy. The number of classrooms remains low because of the mixed results of the first run. Despite the relatively small increase in the number of schools, the situational experts recommend that an Experiment Committee be struck for each project, since the projects are topically diverse, including engaging children in garbage pick-up days and school-based campaigns for environmental literacy. It is important to note that it is not the particular projects themselves that are under investigation, but the impact of the project on student learning.

Data collection at the four sites is again exploratory in nature, involving student interviews and observations, and is again focused on learning gains among grade 7 science students; the related course requirement is a standard question-and-answer test on environmental protection. Pre-service teachers on practica at the four schools serve as fieldworkers gathering observational data using a rubric. The results again support the use of CSL as pedagogy to address the behavioural aspects of those studying environmental education. The students indicate a strong belief that they have changed as a result of the experience. Another rather serendipitous finding is the quality of learning available to teachers-in-training through community service; they get to know the classroom teacher, students, and community in a way not ordinarily possible in a standard practicum. Several post-secondary schools with teacher education programs take notice, and begin deliberations on a partnership arrangement that links standard practica with CSL modules.

The final report recommends a third, larger run, tying the CSL component to pre-service teacher practica. Adding the locations of their various practica broadens the possible research contexts to include rural settings, single-sex schools, and schools with teaching staff who are new to teaching. Classrooms continue to be recruited according to the pre-existing environmental education theme. In the end, thirty classrooms are enlisted, with five categories of diverse environmental protection contexts, ranging from the maintenance of a local boulevard just outside school grounds to a wild animal habitat threatened by development in resort towns. Experiment committees are struck for each project, with members from the Implementation Department sitting on each one. Again assessments of the quality of the individual research studies make it possible to adjust the methods according to the needs of the locations involved. However, adjustments cannot fix a project designed to involve students in cross-cultural dialogue on garbage in the alleys of urban neighbourhoods. The issue is more complex and emotionally fraught than anticipated, and garbage placement and removal prevents the project from moving forward. In the end, the experimental sites are reduced by one.

The results of this larger run reveal that student learning is most enhanced when the environmental protection activity under study reinforces pre-existing concerns in the household. For example, if neighbourhood beautification is a prominent dinner table topic, student involvement in a beautification project leads to significantly better learning.

Normatization. Using CSL to encourage environmental citizenship is subsequently normatized among upper-level elementary students, with some qualifiers. Curriculum designers are apprised of this status by the Knowledge Department and encouraged by policy makers supporting the environmental education theme to include it in their curricula. A teacher training manual describing and promoting CSL is published and disseminated to teacher education programs. A volume of the Epistemic Division's journal – call it *Constant Reform: An International Journal of Educational Redesign* – is dedicated to the topic, and includes the findings of the most exemplary projects. An electronic version of a Handbook of Best Practices includes this innovation.

Summing up. This example illustrates a proposal generated by members of a community organization who attend a regular, local adaptive education consultation. The proposal was co-authored by teachers in a school with a strong can-do culture. The Epistemic Division called in additional resources, including supportive international researchers, pre-service teacher practica, and a graduate student. The example also portrays the ability of thirty classrooms to be involved with particularistic interests in environmental protection, all testing the same pedagogical method – in this case, CSL. The amount of knowledge generated at this scale is important to the eventual normatization of the idea, including its publication in the Handbook of Best Practices.

The presence of a mandated environmental education theme is also an important aspect of this example. The theme came from government officials who had their own objectives in mind, and the adaptive education institution was able to buttress these goals with the Epistemic Division model. Since, in this example, the adaptive education institution also received outside support and resources to improve educational quality through research, the buttressing worked in both directions; community and local government also supported the institution.

7 Conclusion

Public education has evolved in limited ways to meet societal needs since its introduction in the nineteenth century, but it has failed to keep up with modern demands for evidence-based practice. Although many professions base their practice on scientific evidence, education features increasingly separate practitioner and research communities. This widely recognized fact keeps dedicated educators from serving individual learners and the broader society as well as they might, something commentators have recognized for a century.[1] Our institutions allow – even encourage – teachers and administrators to base their practice on instincts or "gut feelings," rather than on evidence, but how can we instil an evidence-based, experimental mindset and respect for scientific method in our educational system? In this book we have proposed an answer.

The principal component of our proposal is a new model, adaptive education, and an institutional structure, the Epistemic Division. Together these posit a way to manage and evaluate on-site experimentation and engage teachers and school administrators in research arising from local problems. Central to this proposed structure are formal procedures and the involvement of experts at every stage of the process to ensure that the research design is sound, the analysis is thorough, and positive results are widely shared and implemented. Using already-existing evidence to establish a level of confidence in proposed interventions, experts would be able to design and scale experiments appropriately, thereby maximizing the potential to enhance students' educational experiences and minimizing risks to both students and the institution. In addition to the potential classroom benefits of new and emerging educational practices, such a system would expose young students to methods of inquiry as a natural part of the learning process in a variety of contexts – personal, classroom, and community. Encouraging local practitioners to identify issues and participate in the design and implementation of experiments would introduce a scientific ethos to the heart of the educational system, an ethos that would be reflected in pre-service teacher education as expectations grow that participation in research is integral to the profession.

Although our proposals are concrete, the underlying theoretical principles emerge in pragmatist theory, as exemplified by John Dewey, Mary Parker Follett, and C.S. Peirce, and more recently by Michael Dorf, Charles Sabel, and Roberto Unger. Pragmatism argues that all human activity is directed towards learning and is "experimental" in nature, and that the knowledge base of individuals relies on their responses to life experiences and the habits of behaviour they develop over time. When we argue that institutions can benefit from installing a local structure and running local experiments to test their ideas and assumptions, we are proposing to expand the range of life experience available to an institution and to create new possibilities for organizational learning and reform.

This would, of course, involve a period of transition for the institution as a whole and for its individual members. If managed well, this would be a healthy introduction to the concept of continuous reform, in which educational institutions are responsive both to changes in their environments and to an ever-evolving and expanding bank of evidence.

Where should we go from here? To start, let us make it clear that the adaptive education model offers extensive benefits to all levels of our educational system. That said, we believe that higher education has the most to prove and to gain by initiating an adaptive education pilot project. We say this because of the perception that research is at best a hit-and-miss proposition, and that too much curiosity-driven research lacks legitimacy. And yet, as we have taken pains to explain, some of the most innovative pedagogies, such as community service learning, call for the incorporation of the real world into the classroom. Another reason for higher education to initiate such a pilot project is its access to resources. Indeed, it would be a fairly simple process to conduct research on the adaptive education model in a university with educational researchers, pre-service teacher programs, and a Faculty of Education with ties to various districts, government ministries, and the broader community. Moreover, the entire structure of the post-secondary realm is quite flexible, making it fairly simple to embed a research team in a course that addressed a school-based problem. In addition, teacher education programs include practica as part of their training and, timed properly, they would provide fieldworkers and other resources.

Given this capacity and efficiency, the ideal next steps could include a pilot research project in a pre-service teachers' program that reflected the adaptive education model. Locating pilot research in such a program would make it possible to study a topic relevant to education in a milieu with abundant resources. At the very least, pre-service teachers would be a good starting point because future teachers represent the potential promise of the model and they would provide easy access to important formative evaluation feedback, which would be available for both the project and the overall idea.

A main goal of the pilot would be to test the various parts of the Epistemic Division, so all pieces should be in place. It would be important to have the various departments work to uncover challenges that could reflect on the Epistemic Division's overall responsiveness. For example, the Knowledge Department could question a research idea that was generated in unconventional way, while the Analysis Department could question the scope of the research. To address these and other concerns, the Experiment Committee could, for example, combine a variety of experts who potentially would complement one another. Regular training programs for course facilitators could include feedback on specific elements of the project, and the additional data would be passed along to researchers affiliated with the project. If the feedback suggested a problem, the researchers could offer quick fixes based on the literature.

The beginnings of a Handbook of Best Practices, or some alternative that accomplished the same function, should also be included in the pilot project. More importantly, we need to find ways to gather feedback on how such a collection could begin to help teachers diagnose their issues. One valuable but provisional step in this direction would be to collect ideas from people on the ground. One of the authors has ventured to do this in co-teaching an urban sustainability course over several years. Using the participatory planning technique of a workshop, students worked on research projects that helped to build an urban trail. Municipal government officials, non-governmental organizations, social service agencies, citizens, and other professionals facilitated the creation and development of these projects, then aided in their evaluation. The projects were conducted over several iterations of the course, which enhanced their legitimacy as well as stakeholder interest, and provided a body of results for teacher use. Feedback from such projects could also be made available through regular open houses or town halls.

A second, relatively simple step would be to implement a mechanism to share best practices. This would involve the creation of venues for collecting feedback from various teaching professionals about the success of different interventions in the classroom. A combination of these two strategies would take the form of an inter-institutional dialogue on education that would include well-respected contributors with reputations for expansive thinking. District researchers, for example, could juxtapose their dream projects with those of a faculty complement, and together they could determine their resonance with local schools. All three voices would provide a gentle nudge towards the development of new professional standards for teachers in a new, data-driven direction.

This relatively cautious start likely would still generate numerous obstacles to overcome before the systematic collaboration necessary for adaptive education became ingrained, as can be quickly appreciated considering the actors involved – university and school board officials, researchers, community members, teachers, students, and parents. School board and university officials likely would balk at the program implications of working closely with one another, citing history as evidence of the success of the status quo. "Students have learned and teachers have taught," officials might say, thus making this relatively measured overture to structural reform a difficult one. It is especially important to note that school board officials would argue that they already make substantial contributions to teacher training through cooperating teachers and students' practica. In addition, this first step would demand a modicum of increased funding to support the participation of the school board and others. Of course, this would fall on shoulders of government, and thus the taxpayer.

We have been careful to describe the implementation of adaptive education in terms of a series of small-scale approaches. Still there is no doubt that the adaptive education model would interest the media and thereby generate questions. The risk, of course, is incurring notoriety before the broader community has had a chance to get involved, gain trust, and, we hope, offer its perspectives. Researchers, especially newer ones, would be key participants in the first steps we propose, and it bears repeating that one hurdle to prioritizing their participation is that they might be asked to study ideas generated by others. As we have noted, researchers value autonomy, and this, too, would be lost in the kind of collaboration called for in the adaptive education model. As well, students and their parents would stand to gain or lose a great deal, and their confidence and support would be pivotal.

In the end, we argue that adaptive education is a flexible, evidence-based approach, and one congruent with the massive resources at our disposal in the form of research infrastructure. It would alleviate the pressure of a reform-oriented dialogue constrained by expectations to "get it right the first time" by acknowledging the reality of adjustment and change. Our goal in writing this book is to inspire the burgeoning discussion of educational reform to include student achievement, teacher satisfaction, more effective social programs, and national competitiveness. By reimagining our educational system to make gathering and applying research-based evidence a driving force, we would move closer to achieving those benefits in the near future. Looking ahead, imagine all of us invested in a public education system that no longer exemplified the rigidity of a staid, if not anachronistic, institution, one that instead was guided by educational practices that evolve to meet changing social realities. In this preferred future, education would rival our society's most innovative institutions by engaging in its own brand of crowdsourcing, creating its own stories of challenge and ascendance, and becoming an important source of responses to growing problems such as sustainability, intercultural conflict, and economic development.

Notes

1 Introduction

1 There are a couple of assumptions here that we address in this book. The first is that policy makers rely heavily on empirical data. The second is that there is a significant correlation between professional development and student performance outcomes.
2 We should also immediately note that we do not take up the parallel question of educational efficiency, at least in terms of cost-efficiency. There is no doubt that education systems around the world, and at all levels, are facing budget crunches and are likely to experience considerable reform in the near future. But this goes beyond the purview of this project.
3 These claims have been made before. See, especially, Hargreaves (1996, 1997). Compare with Campbell (1969).
4 Dewey (1929/2008); Royce (1891); Thorndike (1906).
5 Lortie (1975).
6 Compare with Hayek (1980); Putnam (1992).
7 For an excellent overview of the history involved, see Melton (2003).
8 Although the country fell to French rule, France left the Prussian government in control, albeit in puppet status.
9 Dewey (1916/2008); Gutmann (1987); Lave & Wenger (1991); Locke (1693/2007); Rousseau (1762/1979); Vygotsky (1978).
10 OECD (2013).

2 The Foundations of an Evidence-Based Institution

1 This is something school systems around the world already recognize and avidly pursue. Perhaps the most notable examples of this are special

education programs for children with developmental challenges, and advanced classes and streams for more prepared students.

2 Peirce (1877). There was no solid consensus among the early pragmatists on what to call the state we move into when we become less doubtful. Peirce called it "belief," but Dewey later chastised this position, for good reasons that we do not explore here, and called the end state "warranted assertability." It is hard to tell if any agreement developed over time as pragmatism became more diffuse and was incorporated into a number of fields, since the meaning and scope given to the philosophical tradition changed as it entered new disciplines. For the purposes of this book, these terminological differences do not matter much. We use belief, knowledge, and warranted assertability interchangeably for the end state of inquiry.

3 Dewey (1938/2008).

4 Dewey (1922/2008); Peirce (1878).

5 James (1902/1985).

6 Cooley (1902); James (1890/1981); Thomas & Thomas (1928).

7 Part of pragmatism's enduring influence in the social sciences owes to its view of the self. Our personality and identity are the culmination of countless intersecting habits. See Mead (1934) for the most important work in this regard. Dewey, for his part, presumed a social context for the formation of habits. Without being able to observe or talk to family, friends, or other role models, learning how to problem solve (and to form new habits on that basis) would be extremely difficult. Language, in particular, is a key building block for this cultural matrix, something Dewey discussed at length in his 1929 work, *Logic: The Theory of Inquiry*, but also in earlier work. In the first place language is the main device through which we are able to communicate our ideas to others. But, like many social scientists after him went on to suggest, Dewey noted that language is also an important cognitive tool, one necessary to put certain kinds of thoughts together. Without language, deliberation suffers, which, in turn, affects the process of habit formation. See Johnston (2014) for a discussion of how this comes up in Dewey's work before *Logic*.

8 Dalton (2004); Joas (1996).

9 Dewey (1922/2008).

10 Unger (1987).

11 Joas (1996).

12 Dewey (1938/2008).

13 See Dewey (1922/2008).

14 Dewey (1929/2008); see also McBride (2006).

15 Dewey (1927/2008).

16 Pound (1911).

17 The most basic challenge is one we are all familiar with: people acting
     on behalf of groups have dual interests. They are, on the one hand,
     self-interested and, on the other hand, looking out for the public good
     (however large the relevant public might be). It is no surprise that early
     pragmatists asserted that systems of government were only representative
     to the extent that they encouraged the latter and discouraged the former.
     Bureaucracy and institutionalization help to assuage this trouble, but it is
     not the kind of thing we can ever realistically eliminate.
18 Follett (1918).
19 Brabham (2008). Crowdsourcing has been used successfully in a number of
     contexts. It is now a stock-and-trade method for locating missing persons
     in the wake of disasters, with several websites and government hotlines
     dedicated to the task.
20 See Surowiecki (2005) for an accessible discussion of these findings.
21 Tsoukas (1996).
22 Dewey (1922/2008); Peirce (1878).
23 Dewey (1929/2008); Joas (1996).
24 Follett (1918, p. 33).
25 Mead (1934).
26 The numbers here are somewhat arbitrary, as there is no "magic" number
     for what it means to be big or small.
27 Dewey (1927/2008, p. 306).

3 The Search for a Blueprint

 1 Dorf & Sabel (1998); Unger (1987).
 2 For more about the history of the laboratory school at the University of
     Chicago, see Tanner (1997).
 3 Kilpatrick (1951).
 4 Follett (1918).
 5 There is experimental evidence to support this idea as well; see Blinder &
     Morgan (2000) and its replication by the Bank of England in Lombardelli,
     Proudman, & Talbot (2002).
 6 Putnam (2007) set off the latest maelstrom by showing that diverse
     neighborhoods lead people to be less trusting not only of people in other
     racial and ethnic groups, but also of those in one's own group.
 7 Bilton (2006)
 8 Horton, Kohl, & Kohl (1997); cf. Follett (1918).
 9 Unger (1987).
10 Dorf & Sabel (1998).

11 Hamill & Melis (2012).
12 Susskind, Camacho, & Schenk (2010).
13 Allen (2012).
14 Kuhn (1962).
15 See Campbell (1969)
16 Argyris & Schön (1978); see also Cyert & March (1963).
17 Unger (1987).
18 Utterback & Abernathy (1975).
19 Kuhn (1962).
20 Unger (1987). It is also interesting to compare this to Senge (2006), who articulates an idealized notion of the learning organization that continually capitalizes on the information available to it. Senge identifies certain characteristics that such an organization would need to have, but because he is mainly concerned with making the organizational learning literature more accessible to business leaders, he only teases at more comprehensive answers.

4 Designing an Inquiring Institution

1 Most prominently, Campbell (1969).
2 That is, Baltimore, Boston, Chicago, Los Angeles, and New York City.
3 For more about the study's design, see Shroder & Orr (2012).
4 Put with a little more detail, moving had no effect on adult economic self-sufficiency or physical health, and adolescent males actually experienced adverse effects in terms of physical health and delinquency. Meanwhile, adult mental health improved, and there were significant positive effects for female adolescents almost across the board. Young girls also showed less delinquency.
5 For example, Clampet-Lundquist & Massey (2008); Ludwig et al. (2008).
6 Sampson (2008).
7 Baicker & Finkelstein (2011); Baicker et al. (2013).
8 Cf. Allen (2012).
9 Gross (2009); Schneiderhan (2011)
10 See Ansell (2011, 2012) for much longer takes on this point.
11 Spady, Marshall, & Rogers (1994, p. 30).
12 See, for example, Bayes (1764); de Laplace (1820); Earman (1992); Eells & Fitelson (2000); Jaynes (2003); and Keynes (1921).
13 Goldman (1999).
14 See, for example, Kitcher (1990, 1993); Seidenfeld, Kadane, & Schervish(1989); and Shapley & Grofman (1984).
15 For example, Rasmussen (1975).

16 Cf. Bhatt (2001); Choi & Lee (2002); Chow & Chan (2008); Civi (2000); Davenport & Prusak (1998); Ndlela & du Toit (2001); Nonaka & Takeuchi (1995); and O'Leary (1998).

17 On the relationship between education and poverty, see Apple (1982); Ladd (2012); and Pascarella & Terenzini (1991). On the effects of schooling on health, see Johnson et al. (2010); Lodi-Smith et al. (2010); and Ross & Wu (1995). On the links between education and national economic success, see Acemoglu, Johnson, & Robinson (2001); Hanushek (2005); and Hanushek & Woessmann (2008). Education also affects individual economic outcomes; see Card (1999); Heckman, Lochner, & Todd (2006); and Mincer (1970).

18 Technically, a type I error rejects the null hypothesis when in reality it is correct, and a type II error does not reject the null hypothesis when in reality it is false.

19 An entire literature dedicated to adaptive management tries to do just this.

5 Learning to Teach

1 See, for example, Dewey (1916/2008, 1938/2008).

2 See for example, Lewin (1947); Piaget (1970); Vygotsky (1978).

3 James (1890/1981).

4 See Belliveau (2007); Mayhew & Edwards (1936).

5 Orion (1993); Scarce (1997).

6 Savery (2006) provides an excellent overview of how problem-based learning has been conceptualized in these diverse areas.

7 For example, Hmelo-Silver (2004); Savery & Duffy (1995).

8 VanWynsberghe & Andruske (2007); VanWynsberghe & Moore (2008).

9 For example, Maybach (1996); Savan & Sider (2003); Weinberg (2003).

10 Kebebe, Sheleme, & Wondimu (2007); Vaarst et al. (2007); van den Berg & Knols (2006).

11 Dewey outlines his understanding of childhood in *The Child and the Curriculum* (1902/2008).

12 Knowles (1973). For anyone familiar with the field, it almost goes without saying that pragmatism has been vital to the development of adult education. Along with the influence of Dewey, some of the most prominent contributions have come from Malcolm Knowles, whom very few people associate with pragmatism. His book *The Adult Learner* expanded the snippets of writing devoted to adult education by early pragmatists into a full-blown pedagogical theory. Having read general work by Dewey and Piaget, Knowles developed the concept of andragogy (education of adults), which contrasts itself with pedagogy (education of children).

He emphasized the role of discussion and collaboration in the classroom, partly because adult learners are less dependent on the instructor than children are, and also because these methods tap into the collective life experience of the participants. Since life experience is one of the major resources adults possess, it makes sense to capitalize on it in the classroom. Changes in self-reliance and life experience also entail new relationships to learning. For instance, Knowles argued that adults approach learning for immediate dividends. He believed this was largely conditioned by Western traditions in education, where younger students are told to value the long-term benefits of their learning. The implication is that, once you are engaged in independent economic life, you need to learn for the here-and-now. Andragogy takes advantage of this reality by tailoring the educational experience to the needs of each student. Adults are also self-motivated when they approach education. Again, Knowles believed this has more to do with socialization into independence than with natural tendency. This is the second reason for basing adult education in the real-life challenges of students.

13 Sabel, Saxenian, Miettinen, Kristensen, & Hautamäki (2010).
14 Compare this to the possibility of mini-constitutions of limited scope that could be enacted at the discretion of local actors; see Unger (1987, p. 461).
15 Chetty, Friedman, & Rockoff (2011).
16 Kane, McCaffrey, Miller, & Staiger (2013).
17 Darling-Hammond (2000, 2006); Darling-Hammond & Snyder (2000).
18 Griffin (1989); Loughran & Northfield (2003).
19 Windschitl (2005).
20 Gerofsky (2011).
21 Organisation for Economic Co-operation and Development (1995).
22 Goffman (1959).
23 Lave & Wenger (1991).
24 Jackson (1968); Joyce & Showers (1980).
25 Beck (1992); Giddens (1999).

6 The Role of the Epistemic Division

1 Heathcote & Herbert (1985).
2 For example, Gerofsky (2011).
3 Some people call it STEAM to include the arts or the environment. STEM is a recognition of the close disciplinary ties these fields have to one another and of the importance of interdisciplinary training in these fields.
4 The iTunes platform is being specially modified to allow delocalized

students to ask and answer questions even to the point of stopping the lecture if, for example, a concept is not clear.

5 A percentage of the curricular materials is changed. The hands-on materials will be replaced with electronic ones, and group work and other participatory
·   elements will also be changed. The point is to construct a lecture that is accompanied by a live chat, making it possible to handle questions as they arise.

6 This shift to smaller classes runs counter to the Epistemic Division's emphasis on scaling up, but we believe this will tend to happen when interventions fail (but research does not).

7 Another way to look at this project is to suppose it was not linked to a theme. In all likelihood, if successful at all, the funding would be minimal, perhaps supporting one day of the training of school monitors. Having said this, if its success led to an expansion of this idea for the second round of experimentation and it coincided with environmental protection as a priority, then more resources would be made available to this inaugural project. Indeed, the project could serve a leadership role in the theme itself, continuing to "push the envelope" in the interests of generating useful findings for the other projects.

8 It bears repeating that the Review Board purely reviews the proposal, while the pairing experts can amend the proposals.

9 This goal is experimental in part because addressing behavioural change bumps up against the cherished neutrality of the school. Having said this, schools have embraced some desired social changes, leading to questions about what kinds of social change can be pursued in schools.

10 In fact, early efforts using the Epistemic Division model would be well served by examining the overall process, which would mean evaluating the three departments involved and their relationships with one another, other social institutions, and idea generators. This preliminary work would have to be done in relationship to the literatures on organizational change and partnership development, to name two.

7 Conclusion

1 Dewey (1929/2008); Thorndike (1906).

Works Cited

Acemoglu, D., Johnson, S., & Robinson, J. (2001). The colonial origins of comparative development: An empirical investigation. *American Economic Review, 91*(5), 1369–401. http://dx.doi.org/10.1257/aer.91.5.1369

Allen, B. (2012). Experiments in democracy. *Contemporary Pragmatism, 9*(2), 75–92. http://dx.doi.org/10.1163/18758185-90000231

Ansell, C. (2011). *Pragmatist democracy: Evolutionary learning as public philosophy.* New York, NY: Oxford University Press.

– (2012). What is a "democratic experiment"? *Contemporary Pragmatism, 9*(2), 159–80. http://dx.doi.org/10.1163/18758185-90000235

Apple, M. (1982). *Cultural and economic reproduction in education: Essays on class, ideology, and the state.* New York, NY: Routledge & Kegan Paul.

Argyris, C., & Schön, D. (1978). *Organizational learning: A theory of action perspective.* Reading, MA: Addison Wesley.

Baicker, K., & Finkelstein, A. (2011). The effects of Medicaid coverage: Learning from the Oregon experiment. *New England Journal of Medicine, 365*(8), 683–5. http://dx.doi.org/10.1056/NEJMp1108222

Baicker, K., Taubman, S., Allen, H., Bernstein, M., Gruber, J., Newhouse, J., . . . Finkelstein, A. (2013). The Oregon experiment: Effects of Medicaid on clinical outcomes. *New England Journal of Medicine, 368*(18), 1713–22. http://dx.doi.org/10.1056/NEJMsa1212321

Bayes, T. (1764). An essay towards solving a problem in the doctrine of chances. *Philosophical Transactions of the Royal Society of London, 53,* 370–418.

Beck, U. (1992). *Risk society: Towards a new modernity.* London: Sage.

Belliveau, C. (2007). *A new look at Dewey's cooking lab: A pedagogical model for interdisciplinary learning in contemporary education* (Dissertation). University of Vermont, Educational Leadership and Policy Studies.

Bhatt, G. (2001). Knowledge management in organizations: Examining the interaction between technologies, techniques, and people. *Journal of Knowledge Management, 5*(1), 68–75. http://dx.doi.org/10.1108/13673270110384419

Bilton, C. (2006). Jane Addams, pragmatism, and cultural policy. *International Journal of Cultural Policy, 12*(2), 135–50. http://dx.doi.org/10.1080/10286630600813644

Blinder, A., & Morgan, J. (2000). *Are two heads better than one? An experimental analysis of group vs. individual decisionmaking* (NBER Working Paper 7909). Cambridge, MA: National Bureau of Economic Research.

Brabham, D. (2008). Crowdsourcing as a model for problem solving. *Convergence: The International Journal of Research into New Media Technologies, 14*(1), 75–90. http://dx.doi.org/10.1177/1354856507084420

Campbell, D. (1969). Reforms as experiments. *American Psychologist, 24*(4), 409–29. http://dx.doi.org/10.1037/h0027982

Card, D. (1999). Causal effect of education on earnings. In O. Aschenfelter & D. Card (Eds.), *Handbook of labor economics* (pp. 1801–63). Amsterdam: North Holland.

Chetty, R., Friedman, J., & Rockoff, J. (2011). *The long-term impacts of teachers: Teacher value-added and student outcomes in adulthood* (NBER Working Paper 17699). Cambridge, MA: National Bureau of Economic Research.

Choi, B., & Lee, H. (2002). Knowledge management strategy and its link to knowledge creation process. *Expert Systems with Applications, 23*(3), 173–87. http://dx.doi.org/10.1016/S0957-4174(02)00038-6

Chow, W., & Chan, L. (2008). Social network, social trust, and shared goals in organizational knowledge sharing. *Information & Management, 45*(7), 458–65. http://dx.doi.org/10.1016/j.im.2008.06.007

Civi, E. (2000). Knowledge management as a competitive asset: A review. *Marketing Intelligence & Planning, 18*(4), 166–74. http://dx.doi.org/10.1108/02634500010333280

Clampet-Lundquist, S., & Massey, D. (2008). Neighborhood effects on economic self-sufficiency: A reconsideration of the Moving to Opportunity experiment. *American Journal of Sociology, 114*(1), 107–43. http://dx.doi.org/10.1086/588740

Cooley, C. H. (1902). *Human nature and the social order*. New York, NY: Scribner's.

Cyert, R., & March, J. (1963). *Behavioral theory of the firm* (2nd ed.). Malden, MA: Wiley-Blackwell.

Dalton, B. (2004). Creativity, habit, and the social products of creative action: Revising Joas, incorporating Bourdieu. *Sociological Theory, 22*(4), 603–22. http://dx.doi.org/10.1111/j.0735-2751.2004.00236.x

Darling-Hammond, L. (2000). How teacher education matters. *Journal of Teacher Education, 51*(3), 166–73. http://dx.doi.org/10.1177/0022487100051003002

– (2006). Constructing 21st-century teacher education. *Journal of Teacher Education, 57*(3), 300–14. http://dx.doi.org/10.1177/0022487105285962

Darling-Hammond, L., & Snyder, J. (2000). Authentic assessment of teaching in context. *Teaching and Teacher Education, 16*(5-6), 523–45. http://dx.doi.org/10.1016/S0742-051X(00)00015-9

Davenport, T., & Prusak, L. (1998). *Working knowledge: How organizations manage what they know.* Boston, MA: Harvard Business School Press.

de Laplace, P.-S. (1820). *Théorie analytique des probabilités.* Paris: Gauthier-Villars.

Dewey, J. (2008). The middle works of John Dewey (Vol. 2). *The child and the curriculum.* Carbondale; Edwardsville, IL: Southern Illinois University Press. (Original work published 1902).

– (2008). The middle works of John Dewey (Vol. 9). *Democracy and education.* Carbondale; Edwardsville, IL: Southern Illinois University Press. (Original work published 1916).

– (2008). The middle works of John Dewey (Vol. 14). *Human nature and conduct.* Carbondale; Edwardsville, IL: Southern Illinois University Press. (Original work published 1922).

– (2008). The later works of John Dewey (Vol. 2). *Essays, reviews, miscellany, and the public and its problems.* Carbondale; Edwardsville, IL: Southern Illinois University Press. (Original work published 1927).

– (2008). The later works of John Dewey (Vol. 5). *Essays, the sources of a science of education, individualism, old and new, and construction and criticism.* Carbondale; Edwardsville, IL: Southern Illinois University Press. (Original work published 1929).

– (2008). The later works of John Dewey (Vol. 13). *Experience and education, freedom and culture, theory of valuation, and essays.* Carbondale; Edwardsville, IL: Southern Illinois Press. (Original work published 1938).

Dorf, M., & Sabel, C. (1998). A constitution of democratic experimentalism. *Columbia Law Review, 98*(2), 267–473. http://dx.doi.org/10.2307/1123411

Earman, J. (1992). *Bayes or bust? A critical examination of Bayesian confirmation theory.* Cambridge, MA: MIT Press.

Eells, E., & Fitelson, B. (2000). Measuring confirmation and evidence. *Journal of Philosophy, 97*(12), 663–72. http://dx.doi.org/10.2307/2678462

Follett, M. (1918). *The new state: Group organization the solution of popular government.* University Park, PA: Pennsylvania State University.

Gerofsky, S. (2011). Seeing the graph vs. being the graph: Gesture, engagement, and awareness in school mathematics. In G. Stam & M. Ishino (Eds.), *Integrating gestures* (pp. 245–56). Amsterdam: John Benjamins.

Giddens, A. (1999). Risk and responsibility. *Modern Law Review, 62*(1), 1–10. http://dx.doi.org/10.1111/1468-2230.00188

Goffman, E. (1959). *The presentation of self in everyday life*. New York, NY: Doubleday.

Goldman, A.I. (1999). *Knowledge in a social world*. Oxford, UK: Clarendon Press. http://dx.doi.org/10.1093/0198238207.001.0001

Griffin, G. A. (1989). A descriptive study of student teaching. *Elementary School Journal, 89*(3), 343–64. http://dx.doi.org/10.1086/461579

Gross, M. (2009). Collaborative experiments: Jane Addams, Hull House, and experimental social work. *Social Sciences Information, 48*(1), 81–95. http://dx.doi.org/10.1177/0539018408099638

Gutmann, A. (1987). *Democratic education*. Princeton, NJ: Princeton University Press.

Hamill, J., & Melis, T. (2012). The Glen Canyon Dam Adaptive Management Program: Progress and immediate challenges. In P. Boon & P. Raven (Eds.), *River conservation and management* (pp. 325–38). New York, NY: John Wiley & Sons. http://dx.doi.org/10.1002/9781119961819.ch26

Hanushek, E. (2005). *Economic outcomes and school quality*. Paris: UNESCO, International Institute for Educational Planning.

Hanushek, E., & Woessmann, L. (2008). The role of cognitive skills in economic development. *Journal of Economic Literature, 46*(3), 607–68. http://dx.doi.org/10.1257/jel.46.3.607

Hargreaves, D. (1996). *Teaching as a research-based profession: Possibilities and prospects*. The Teacher Training Agency Annual Lecture, 1996. London.

– (1997). In defense of evidence-based teaching: A rejoinder to Martyn Hammersly. *British Educational Research Journal, 23*(4), 405–19. http://dx.doi.org/10.1080/0141192970230402

Hayek, F. (1980). *The counter-revolution of science: Studies on the abuse of reason*. Indianapolis, IN: Liberty Fund.

Heathcote, D., & Herbert, P. (1985). A drama of learning: Mantle of the expert. *Theory into Practice, 24*(3), 173–80. http://dx.doi.org/10.1080/00405848509543169

Heckman, J., Lochner, L., & Todd, P. (2006). Earnings functions, rates of returns and treatment effects: The Mincer equation and beyond. In E. Hanushek & F. Welch (Eds.), *Handbook of the economics of education* (pp. 307–458). Amsterdam: North Holland. http://dx.doi.org/10.1016/S1574-0692(06)01007-5

Hmelo-Silver, C. (2004). Problem-based learning: What and how do students learn? *Educational Psychology Review, 16*(3), 235–66. http://dx.doi.org/10.1023/B:EDPR.0000034022.16470.f3

Horton, M., Kohl, J., & Kohl, H. (1997). *The long haul: An autobiography*. New York, NY: Teachers College Press.

Jackson, P. (1968). *Life in classrooms*. New York, NY: Teachers College Press.

James, W. (1981). Principles of psychology (Vol. I). *II*. Cambridge, MA: Harvard University Press. (Original work published 1890).

– (1985). *The varieties of religious experience.* Cambridge, MA: Harvard University Press. (Original work published 1902).

Jaynes, E. T. (2003). *Probability theory: The logic of science.* Cambridge, UK: Cambridge University Press. http://dx.doi.org/10.1017/CBO9780511790423

Joas, H. (1996). *The creativity of action.* Chicago, IL: University of Chicago Press.

Johnson, W., Kyvik, K., Mortensen, E., Skytthe, A., Batty, G., & Deary, I. (2010). Education reduces the effects of genetic susceptibilities to poor physical health. *International Journal of Epidemiology, 39*(2), 406–14. http://dx.doi.org/10.1093/ije/dyp314

Johnston, J. (2014). *John Dewey's earlier logical theory.* New York, NY: SUNY Press.

Joyce, B., & Showers, B. (1980). Improving inservice training: The messages of research. *Educational Leadership, 35*(5), 379–85.

Kane, T., McCaffrey, D., Miller, T., & Staiger, D. (2013). *Have we identified effective teachers? Validating measures of effective teaching using random assignment* (MET Project Research Paper). Seattle, WA: Bill & Melinda Gates Foundation.

Kebebe, E., Sheleme, B., & Wondimu, W. (2007). Learning experiences of farmers field school on integrated nutrient management: Evidence from Wolaita in southern Ethiopia. *Journal of Agronomy, 6*(4), 560–65. http://dx.doi.org/10.3923/ja.2007.560.565

Keynes, J. M. (1921). *A treatise on probability.* London: Macmillan.

Kilpatrick, W. H. (1951). *Philosophy of education.* London: Macmillan.

Kitcher, P. (1990). The division of cognitive labor. *Journal of Philosophy, 87*(1), 5–22. http://dx.doi.org/10.2307/2026796

– (1993). *The advancement of science.* New York, NY: Oxford University Press.

Knowles, M. (1973). *The adult learner: A neglected species.* Houston, TX: Gulf Publishing.

Kuhn, T. (1962). *The structure of scientific revolutions.* Chicago, IL: University of Chicago Press.

Ladd, H. (2012). Education and poverty: Confronting the evidence. *Journal of Policy Analysis and Management, 31*(2), 203–27. http://dx.doi.org/10.1002/pam.21615

Lave, J., & Wenger, E. (1991). *Situated learning: Legitimate peripheral participation.* Cambridge, UK: Cambridge University Press. http://dx.doi.org/10.1017/CBO9780511815355

Lewin, K. (1947). Frontiers in group dynamics: II. Channels of group life; social planning; and action research. *Human Relations, 1*(2), 143–53. http://dx.doi.org/10.1177/001872674700100201

Lodi-Smith, J., Jackson, J., Bogg, T., Walton, K., Wood, D., Harms, P., & Roberts, B. (2010). Mechanisms of health: Education and health-related behaviours partially mediate the relationship between conscientious and self-reported physical health. *Psychology & Health, 25*(3), 305–19. http://dx.doi.org/10.1080/08870440902736964

Locke, J. (2007). *Some thoughts concerning education*. Mineola, NY: Dover Publications. (Original work published 1693).

Lombardelli, C., Proudman, J., & Talbot, J. (2002). *Committees versus individuals: An experimental analysis of monetary policy decision-making* (Working Paper 165). London: Bank of England.

Lortie, D. (1975). *Schoolteacher: A sociological study*. Chicago, IL: University of Chicago Press.

Loughran, J., & Northfield, J. (2003). *Opening the classroom door: Teacher, researcher, learner*. Bristol, PA: Routledge.

Ludwig, J., Liebman, J., Kling, J., Duncan, G., Katz, L., Kessler, R., & Sanbonmatsu, L. (2008). What can we learn about neighborhood effects from the Moving to Opportunity experiment? *American Journal of Sociology, 114*(1), 144–88. http://dx.doi.org/10.1086/588741

Maybach, C. W. (1996). Investigating urban community needs: RSL from a social justice perspective. *Education and Urban Society, 28*(2), 224–36. http://dx.doi.org/10.1177/0013124596028002007

Mayhew, K., & Edwards, A. (1936). *The Dewey school: The Laboratory School of the University of Chicago, 1896–1903*. New York, NY: Appleton-Century.

McBride, L. (2006). Collectivistic individualism: Dewey and MacIntyre. *Contemporary Pragmatism, 3*(1), 69–83. http://dx.doi.org/10.1163/18758185-90000033

Mead, G. H. (1934). *Mind, self, and society: From the standpoint of a social behaviorist*. Chicago, IL: University of Chicago Press.

Melton, J. (2003). *Absolutism and the eighteenth-century origins of compulsory education in Prussia and Austria*. Cambridge, UK: Cambridge University Press.

Mincer, J. (1970). The distribution of labor incomes: A survey with special reference to the human capital approach. *Journal of Economic Literature, 8*(1), 1–26.

Ndlela, L., & du Toit, A. S. A. (2001). Establishing a knowledge management programme for competitive advantage in an enterprise. *International Journal of Information Management, 21*(2), 151–65. http://dx.doi.org/10.1016/S0268-4012(01)00007-X

Nonaka, I., & Takeuchi, H. (1995). *The knowledge-creating company: How Japanese companies create the dynamics of innovation*. New York, NY: Oxford University Press.

Organisation for Economic Co-operation and Development (1995). *Educational research and development: Trends, issues, and challenges*. Paris: OECD Publications.

– (2013). *Education indicators in focus*. Paris: OECD Publications.

O'Leary, D. (1998). Using AI in knowledge management: Knowledge bases and ontologies. *Intelligent Systems and their Applications, 13*(3), 34–9. http://dx.doi.org/10.1109/5254.683180

Orion, N. (1993). A model for the development and implementation of field trips as an integral part of the science curriculum. *School Science and Mathematics, 93*(6), 325–31. http://dx.doi.org/10.1111/j.1949-8594.1993.tb12254.x

Pascarella, T., & Terenzini, P. (1991). *How college affects students: Findings and insights from twenty years of research*. San Francisco, CA: Jossey-Bass.

Peirce, C. (1877). The fixation of belief. *Popular Science Monthly, 12*, 1–12.

– (1878). How to make our ideas clear. *Popular Science Monthly, 12*, 286–302.

Piaget, J. (1970). *Science of education and the psychology of the child*. New York, NY: Orion Press.

Pound, R. (1911). Scope and purpose of sociological jurisprudence. *Harvard Law Review, 25*(2), 140–68. http://.dx.doi.org/10.2307/1324392

Putnam, H. (1992). *Renewing philosophy*. Cambridge, MA: Harvard University Press.

Putnam, R. (2007). E pluribus unum: Diversity and community in the twenty-first century. *Scandinavian Political Studies, 30*(2), 137–74. http://dx.doi.org/10.1111/j.1467-9477.2007.00176.x

Rasmussen, N. C. (1975). *Reactor safety study: An assessment of accident risks in U.S. commercial nuclear power plants*. Washington, DC: United States Nuclear Regulatory Commission.

Ross, C., & Wu, C. (1995). The links between education and health. *American Sociological Review, 60*(5), 719–45. http://dx.doi.org/10.2307/2096319

Rousseau, J. (1979). *Emile, or on education* (A. Bloom, Trans.). New York, NY: Basic Books. (Original work published 1762).

Royce, J. (1891). Is there a science of education? *Educational Review, 1*(1), 15–25.

Sabel, C., Saxenian, A., Miettinen, R., Kristensen, P., & Hautamäki, J. (2010). *Individualized service provision in the new welfare state: Lessons from special education in Finland*. Helsinki: SITRA.

Sampson, R. (2008). Moving to inequality: Neighborhood effects and experiments meet social structure. *American Journal of Sociology, 114*(1), 189–231. http://dx.doi.org/10.1086/589843

Savan, B., & Sider, D. (2003). Contrasting approaches to community-based research: A case study of community sustainability. *Local Environment, 8*(3), 303–16. http://dx.doi.org/10.1080/13549830306657

Savery, J. (2006). Overview of problem-based learning: Definitions and distinctions. *Interdisciplinary Journal of Problem-Based Learning, 1*(1), 9–20. http://dx.doi.org/10.7771/1541-5015.1002

Savery, J., & Duffy, T. (1995). Problem-based learning: An instructional model and its constructivist framework. *Educational Technology, 35*, 31–8.

Scarce, R. (1997). Field trips as short-term experiential education. *Teaching Sociology, 25*(3), 219–26. http://dx.doi.org/10.2307/1319398

Schneiderhan, E. (2011). Pragmatism and empirical sociology: The case of Jane Addams and Hull House, 1880–1895. *Theory and Society, 40*(6), 589–617. http://dx.doi.org/10.1007/s11186-011-9156-2

Seidenfeld, T., Kadane, J., & Schervish, M. (1989). On the shared preferences of two Bayesian decision makers. *Journal of Philosophy, 86*(5), 225–44. http://dx.doi.org/10.2307/2027108

Senge, P. (2006). *The fifth discipline: The art and practice of the learning organization.* New York, NY: Doubleday.

Shapley, L., & Grofman, B. (1984). Optimizing group judgmental accuracy in the presence of interdependence. *Public Choice, 43*(3), 329–43. http://dx.doi.org/10.1007/BF00118940

Shroder, M., & L. Orr. (2012). Moving to opportunity: Why, how, and what next? *Cityscape: A Journal of Policy Development and Research, 14*(2): 31–56.

Spady, W. G., Marshall, K., & Rogers, S. (1994). Light, not heat, OBE. *American School Board Journal, 181*(11), 29–33.

Surowiecki, J. (2005). *The wisdom of crowds.* New York, NY: Anchor Books.

Susskind, L., Camacho, A., & Schenk, T. (2010). Collaborative planning and adaptive management in Glen Canyon: A cautionary tale. *Columbia Journal of Environmental Law, 35*(1), 1–54.

Tanner, L. (1997). *Dewey's laboratory school: Lessons for today.* New York, NY: Teachers College Press.

Thomas, W. I., & Thomas, D. S. (1928). *The child in America: Behavior problems and programs.* New York, NY: Knopf.

Thorndike, E. (1906). *The principles of teaching based on psychology.* New York, NY: A.G. Seiler. http://dx.doi.org/10.1037/11487-000

Tsoukas, H. (1996). The firm as a distributed knowledge system: A constructionist approach. *Strategic Management Journal, 17*(S2), 11–25. http://dx.doi.org/10.1002/smj.4250171104

Unger, R. (1987). *False necessity.* Cambridge, UK: Cambridge University Press.

Utterback, J., & Abernathy, W. (1975). A dynamic model of process and product innovation. *Omega, 3*(6), 639–56. http://dx.doi.org/10.1016/0305-0483(75)90068-7

Vaarst, M., Nissen, T., Østergaard, S., Klaas, I., Bennedsgaard, T., & Christensen, J. (2007). Danish stable schools for experiential common learning in groups of organic dairy farmers. *Journal of Dairy Science, 90*(5), 2543–54. http://dx.doi.org/10.3168/jds.2006-607

van den Berg, H., & Knols, B. (2006). The farmer field school: A method for enhancing the role of rural communities in malaria control? *Malaria Journal*, 5(3), 1–6.

VanWynsberghe, R., & Andruske, C. (2007). Research in the service of co-learning: Sustainability and community engagement. *Canadian Journal of Education*, 30(1), 349–76. http://dx.doi.org/10.2307/20466638

VanWynsberghe, R., & Moore, J. (2008). Envisioning the classroom as a social movement organization. *Policy Futures in Education*, 6(3), 298–311. http://dx.doi.org/10.2304/pfie.2008.6.3.298

Vygotsky, L. (1978). *Mind and society: The development of higher psychological processes*. Cambridge, MA: Harvard University Press.

Weinberg, A. S. (2003). Negotiating community-based research: A case study of the "Life's Work" project. *Michigan Journal of Community Service Learning*, 9(3): 26–35.

Windschitl, M. (2005). The future of science teacher preparation in America: Where is the evidence to inform program design and guide responsible policy decisions? *Science Education*, 89(4), 525–34. http://dx.doi.org/10.1002/sce.20090

Index

Page numbers in italics indicate a figure

educational experimentation. *See* adaptive education

educational institutions. *See* institutions

educational reform: balance of neutrality and social impact, 47; and class size, 46; constant, 43–8; evolving, 21; and institutional design, 78; and length of school day, 46; and school choice, 46. *See also* institutional reform

educational research. *See* adaptive education

Epistemic Division: and adaptive education, 108; buttressing, 83, 107; described, 16–19, 82; and disentrenchment, 48; and educational policy, 92; and ethics, 18; and expansive thinking, 94; governance, 82–3; and local actors, 83; organization of, 83–7, *84*, 119n10; purpose of, 59; role of, 82–107; scaling, 83, 119n6; testing, 110; and universities, 95. *See also* Analysis Department; Implementation Department; Knowledge Department

ethics: in decision-making process, 99; and Epistemic Division, 18; and industry involvement, 96; and inquiry, 56–9; of participation, 59–62

Experiment Committee, *84*, 86, 90–2, 96–7, 101, 103, 105–6, 110

factory model, and education, 6–9

False Necessity, 32, 47

Finland, 9, 64

folk schools, Danish, 37

Follett, Mary Parker: collective

inquiry, 28, 30; group inquiry, 75–6; "group process," 34–5; limits of ideas of, 40; pragmatism, 65, 109; problem solving, 30

Germany, school system of, 8

Gerofsky, Susan, 89–90

Glen Canyon Dam Adaptive Management Program, 41

Goldman, Alvin, 54

government funding, 11–12, 111

group ideas, 35

"group process," 34–5

gut feelings, 4, 108

habits: and adaptation, 22–7, 29; and adult learners, 69; and best practices, 76; and creativity, 26, 67, 77; and decision making, 29; and deliberation, 114n7; and inquiry, 26; and learning, 67, 77, 109; resistance to change, 25; rigid, 25–6; transposing, 24–5

Handbook of Best Practices in Education, 86, 106, 110

harm, potential for, 53, 57–61

health, and education, 13–14

Heathcote, Dorothy, 88–9

Highlander Folk School, 37–8, 76

home schooling, 60, 81

Horton, Myles, 37

Hull House, 36–7

Implementation Department, 83–5, *84*, 86–7, 91, 95–6, 104, 106

Industrial Revolution, and public education, 6

inquiry: and best practices, 53; and collaboration, 57; collective, 28; and democratic experimentalism,